STAMP A

CHRISTIAN
GREETING™

Judy Ritchie, Kate Schmidt,
and Jamie Kilmartin, with John Kelsey
Stamp designs by Judy Pelikan

HUGH LAUTER LEVIN ASSOCIATES, INC.

Copyright © 1999 by Hugh Lauter Levin Associates, Inc.

Stamp designs © 1999 by Judy Pelikan
Line drawings by Susan Swan

All of the *Stamp-A-Christian Greeting*™ projects have been created by Judy Ritchie,
of The Great American Stamp Store in Westport, CT

Printed in Hong Kong
ISBN 0-88363-930-0

Stamp-A-Christian Greeting™ is a trademark of All Night Media, San Rafael, CA,
and is used under license.
All Night Media, Inc., was a pioneer in the art of rubber stamping
and has been creating innovative rubber stamp products for twenty years.
You can find their quality products at gift, toy, craft, and
bookstores nationwide.

Distributed by Publisher's Group West

INTRODUCTION

$\mathcal{A}$ heartfelt Christian greeting will brighten anyone's day. You don't need a special occasion to send a prayer or share your joy. What makes receiving a stamped greeting so special is that it's made with love. It's a wonderful feeling to know that someone has taken the trouble to make a one-of-a-kind greeting just for you.

$\mathcal{Y}$our *Stamp-A-Christian Greeting*™ kit contains images that will help you create appropriate greetings for religious holidays, important events such as baptisms, first communions, and weddings, and for shut-ins and people who are ill. You can also use the stamps and pens in your *Stamp-A-Christian Greeting*™ kit to send greetings for birthdays, graduation from school or college, or just because you feel like giving someone's spirits a lift.

$\mathcal{Y}$ou can let your creativity loose with rubber stamped greetings, and you don't have to be an artist to succeed. With rubber stamp images, you can make your own beautiful artwork, by combining images, and by the way you frame and embellish images as you compose your greetings.

$\mathcal{R}$ubber stamping is a wonderfully satisfying hobby for people of all ages, from children in kindergarten or Sunday school to senior citizens. Once you learn the basics, you'll be able to use your stamps, inks, and pens to create activities for yourself and for your friends. For example, stamping can be a fun birthday party activity, a teaching tool in Church school, or a memorable holiday event. You can use your stamps to show young children how to make greetings that express their thoughts and feelings. And you will find many other good ways to use your stamping skills.

The Stamp-A-Christian Greeting™ kit contains everything you need to get started. Once you learn how to use these basic tools and materials, there are lots more colors and motifs you can use to help send your message to everyone you know. Included in the kit are:

❖ 20 art rubber stamps with Christian themes designed just for this kit

❖ Red and black brush markers

❖ Red, blue, purple, yellow, brown, and green colored pencils

❖ A specially designed template

❖ 6 die-cut place cards

❖ 6 ornaments/charms with gold ties

❖ One pair of decorative-edged scissors

❖ 6 blank white greeting cards with envelopes

Your stamping kit includes the materials and supplies you need to create greeting cards with envelopes, inspirational messages, birthday cards with a Christian theme, wrapping paper, personalized invitations and thank-you notes, get-well cards, and special greetings for Christmas and Easter, as well as other holiday times of the year. You'll be able to express your message on hand-stamped stationery, or with special fabric inks, as on a T-shirt. You'll soon find all kinds of ways to spread the Word with rubber-stamped greetings.

To get off to a good start, it's important that you spend a little time becoming familiar with the basic techniques and tips contained in this handbook. You will find many inspirational ideas in the projects section at the back of the book, too. These projects have been carefully planned and tested, so you're certain to succeed. But you don't have to stop there. You might start with an idea you got from one of our projects, then develop it in your own direction. Don't be afraid to try a project for a second or third time, either. You'll increase your basic skills and build your vocabulary of techniques, and you will find that new ideas come to you as you work.

Soon you will automatically turn to your collection of stamps, pens, and stencils for every special day or event when you normally would buy a greeting card or send a handwritten note. You will be able to stamp cards to commemorate a family baptism, first communion. or confirmation. Along with personalized greetings, you can make place cards for parties and name tags for open houses and other special events. And don't forget about announcements for bulletin boards at school and church.

*Y*ou need not feel confined by the stamps and materials in your kit. This selection has been designed to get you off to a good start. Soon you will want to expand your kit by adding more stamps, more pens, and more special papers and envelopes. You will find some of these materials at specialty stores for rubber stamping, but you will also find many useful things at regular art supply or stationery stores. Look especially for more colors, and for such novelty materials as glitter glue and puffy paint.

*D*on't neglect the materials you probably have already, such as ribbon, tape, stickers, string, buttons, or dried flowers. If you like something, you will no doubt be able to find a creative way to use it in your artwork.

*P*rinting techniques like stamping have a long history of service to Christianity. A set of letter stamps can be used to reproduce a Biblical verse or an inspirational message. Movable type, which was invented early in the sixteenth century, is simply a large set of individual letter-stamps that can be combined to make many different pages of text. When the German printer Johannes Gutenberg invented movable type, one of the first things he printed was the Holy Bible. Before Gutenberg's time, the only way to reproduce a Bible was to copy it by hand. The invention of movable type made it possible for anyone to have his or her own copy of the Bible. When you stamp or stencil an inspirational greeting, you're participating in this tradition.

*W*e hope this book and the kit of materials that comes with it inspires you to try this fascinating hobby. You will delight your friends and family, and you'll probably surprise yourself as your creative abilities unfold. So go ahead and get started, and have some fun!

GETTING STARTED

efore using the rubber stamps in your *Stamp-A-Christian Greeting*™ kit, you must separate them from the block. Break the block of stamps apart at the cuts in the rubber material. The thick foam back functions as a handle that makes it easy to use these stamps. Since you'll want to know which stamp is which, there's a sheet of self-adhesive labels (an index) in your kit.

*P*eel each index off the backing paper and stick it to the foam back of the matching stamp. Position the index carefully, making sure it's straight and oriented the same way as the image on the stamp. Protect the index stickers by covering them with heavy transparent packing tape or clear contact paper. Carefully trim any excess paper or tape flush with the edge of the stamp block.

*S*unlight, heat, and dust are harmful to the rubber in stamps. Leaving the stamps out will make them dry, hard, and unus-

able. Always clean your stamps after each use, and protect them by storing them rubber side down, out of direct sunlight. Store your stamps right in your *Stamp-A-Christian Greeting*™ kit, though once you get into stamping you'll acquire more stamps and inks, and you'll need a bigger container. Translucent

plastic food-storage boxes work well, and so do small cardboard boxes with lids.

As with other craft projects, you need to prepare a comfortable working area. Clear a space on your table or desk, and cover it with a large newsprint pad. Working on a cushioned surface like newsprint gives you the sharpest images. The newsprint also provides a scrap surface for testing images, and it will protect your desk or table from stray ink. If you don't have a clean newsprint pad, use a computer mouse pad or an old magazine as a cushioned work surface, and protect your worktable with yesterday's newspaper.

HOW TO STAMP

The post office clerk can stamp "Air Mail" onto your letter with a mighty whack, because it's not crucial whether the image comes up absolutely clear or not. But when you are creating a personal greeting, you do care. Think of the mark the stamp makes as an imprint, or impression. Making a good impression on paper is like making a good impression in person: be firm and even, and take your time.

There are several ways to ink a stamp, which we'll cover in the next chapter. For now, to get started, tap your stamp onto an ink pad, then carefully position it on your paper. Hold the stamp in position with one hand, while you press evenly on its back with your other hand. Exactly how hard to press depends on the kind of image. Large stamps—and small stamps with large solid areas—require more ink and pressure than finely detailed stamps. Press with your finger tips and move the pressure evenly over the whole back of the stamp. Be careful not to rock or wiggle the stamp, or you will get a blurry image.

Each stamp has its own peculiarities, which you'll discover by stamping test prints on scrap paper or on your newsprint pad. To get a good image, you might have to press harder in one area or another. It's worth experimenting to learn how to get the best results, before you make final prints on your best paper.

When you're making greeting cards, the fold may cause problems, as might

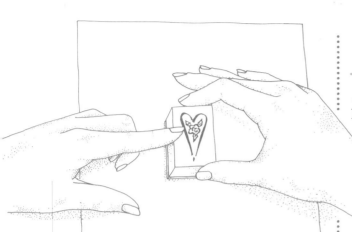

To make a good image, hold the stamp firmly in place with one hand and press it down evenly with the other hand. Move your finger to press all parts of the stamp into contact with the paper.

the glue seams of envelopes. The ink might not stick near the folds and seams. This is why it's important to open each card and lay it flat. You can't do that with an envelope, but you can slip a thin piece of cardboard inside, making a smooth surface. For the best stamping results, it's always worth the time and trouble to take this kind of extra care.

BRUSH MARKERS, PENCILS, AND PAPER

*T*he brush markers included in your kit can be used to draw on all kinds of paper, but you can also use them to ink your stamps. The advantage of inking with brush markers is that you can ink part of a stamp or the whole stamp. You can also ink different parts of the image with different colored markers, to create a multi-colored stamped image.

*A*s you'll see in the Special Projects section of this book, the technique of selective inking helps create many different images and effects from a small number of stamps. Instead of using the word "Joy" together with the rose, you could ink only the letters, or only the flower. You don't have to use the heart, moon, and star together, because you can select and color only the image you want for your project. Also, your stamps can be used to make a single image, or repeatedly to cover the page with pictures, like wrapping paper. Once you've had a little practice, you'll find many creative and different ways to use your stamps and colors.

The brush markers in your kit contain water-based ink. Supplement them with any other water-based markers you might have. To prevent your markers from drying out, be sure to cap them tightly between uses.

Most stampers like the control they can get by directly inking with markers. You can also use stamp pads, as long as they contain only water-based ink (solvent inks may damage your stamps). Tap the rubber stamp gently on the surface of the pad, then test it on scrap paper. You might find that the pad puts more ink than you need onto the stamp, so to get the impression you want stamp first on scrap, then on good paper, without re-inking.

The colored pencils in your kit can add another dimension to your stamping projects. They're ideal for achieving the pleasing effects of soft colors and subtle shading, and they can be used together with all kinds of stamp inks.

There is enough paper in your kit to get you started, and to show you how the paper affects the stamped image. But experiment with many different kinds of paper. You'll soon develop your own personal favorites. And although expensive papers might produce the images you like best, it's not wise to buy a lot of paper "just in case." You'll find that your tastes evolve as you gain experience, so the paper you liked yesterday might not be your favorite today.

Pay particular attention to the difference between stamping on smooth, glossy paper and on matte finished paper, or even on uncoated or textured paper. Each kind of finish absorbs the ink differently. There is no "best" paper for your stamping projects—which ones you choose depends on the effect you have in mind. That's why it pays to experiment, and to keep a folder of your experiments so you can shop for the right effect.

Don't get locked in to the size and shape of the paper in the kit, or what you find in the store. You can cut any paper into shapes you like, then layer several different kinds of paper, make paper frames to set off your images, and make collages out of stamped images, handmade papers, and "found" objects.

CLEANING YOUR STAMPS

*Y*ou'll always get the best results when you start with a clean stamp. Be sure to clean the ink off your stamps after every color change, and before you put them away. The easiest way to do this is to have a cleaning plate ready—that is, a wet paper towel, sponge, or rag on a small plate or saucer. Keep a dry towel or an old T-shirt handy also, to dry your stamps after they have been cleaned.

*B*efore cleaning each stamp, tap it gently on scrap paper to remove as much ink as possible. Tap the stamp onto the cleaning plate several times, then wipe it dry.

*W*ater is the best solvent for cleaning stamps. If there's any stubborn ink in the rubber, try scrubbing it with an old toothbrush dipped in water, then tap on the cleaning plate as usual. If there's any stray glitter embedded in the rubber, lift it off with a loop of sticky tape. Don't use harsh cleaners or alcohol-based solvents, because they'll dry out the rub-

Clean your stamps after every use. Make a cleaning plate by moistening a paper towel, sponge, or rag.

ber and leave a film on it. When you're finished, clean your hands thoroughly with soap and water too.

SUPPLIES YOU WILL NEED

*H*ere are some household and art supplies you'll probably need, so gather them together before you sit down to work:

- Dye ink pad
- Pigment ink pad
- Water-based brush markers
- Paper cutter, scissors, decorative scissors
- Large newsprint pad
- X-Acto knife or mat knife
- Scrap paper
- Plain and colored card stock
- Sticky notes or thin paper for masking
- Cleaning plate with sponge or wet paper towels
- Dry towel or old T-shirt
- Glue
- Envelopes
- Ruler and positioner

SUPPLIES YOU MIGHT WANT

*Y*ou'll soon find that all kinds of art materials can be used in stamping projects. Here are some things you might like to try:

- Colored pencils
- Fine-tipped markers

- Glitter, glitter glue
- Embossing pens, markers, and pads; heat gun or alternative heat source (page 59)
- Acrylic paints (for wood), sandpaper, spray acrylic sealer
- Crack-and-peel (sticker) paper
- Double-stick cellophane tape
- Double-sided foam tape
- Uncoated matte-finish gift wrap
- Plain tissue paper
- Paper punches
- Watercolor pencils, watercolors, brushes
- Soft chalks and pastels
- Sponges and compressed cellulose sponges (page 47)
- Brayers (ink rollers)
- Large rubber eraser or reverse-image stamp
- Fabric paint or ink
- Foam brushes or pads

BASIC INKING TECHNIQUES

Although rubber stamps will work with almost any kind of water-soluble ink or paint, two kinds of ink—dye and pigment—are most suitable. Both kinds of ink come in single-color pads, rainbow ink pads, and in brush markers. You can use ink pads when you want to see the whole image on the stamp in a single color. Use brush markers when you want to see only part of the image on the stamp, when you want to use more than one color at a time, or if inking the stamp itself is the method that you prefer. (This is our favorite way to work.)

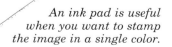

An ink pad is useful when you want to stamp the image in a single color.

Always keep markers and stamp pads closed when they are not in use, so the ink doesn't dry out. Most stamp pads can be re-inked with the same color and type of ink. However, you should not try to re-ink a dye pad with pigment ink or a pigment pad with dye ink, or some other kind of ink. You can also create your own rainbow pads by putting bottled inks on an un-inked felt or foam pad.

INKING WITH A DYE INK PAD

Dye ink is quick drying and it works on almost any kind of paper. Pads of dye ink come in a wide variety of colors. Pads are made so their surface is higher than the edge of the case. This makes it possible for you to cover any size stamp with a small ink pad.

Tap the stamp several times on the pad, then look at it to make sure the ink has wet the entire image. Tap the pad gently. If you tap too hard, you might get ink on the background rubber surrounding the image, which could ruin your project.

$\mathcal{I}$nk your stamps by tapping them onto the ink pad, or by holding the stamp image-up and tapping it with the pad. Try both techniques to see which of these methods you like best.

$\mathcal{D}$ye ink is translucent. This means the color of the paper affects the color of the image. Also, if you stamp a picture in one color over another image in a different color, the bottom image will show through. Use this property to create transparent effects in your artwork. To

*To make a
light impression,
stamp on scrap paper
and then, without re-inking,
stamp again on good paper.*

make a lighter shade of a color, try double-stamping. Ink the stamp, then press it onto a piece of scrap paper before stamping the remaining image on your good paper.

INKING WITH WATER-BASED MARKERS

$\mathcal{B}$rush markers, which contain the same kind of water-soluble ink as dye ink pads, also can be used to ink stamps. With brush markers, you've got total control over which parts of the image to color, and what colors to use. Also, without an ink pad, there's no limit on the size of stamp you can color.

$\mathcal{T}$o ink a stamp with a brush marker, hold the stamp image-up and paint it with as many colors as you like. Brush over the entire area you wish to stamp with the broad side of the marker. When you're using more than one color, start with the lightest and work toward the darkest. This prevents getting darker ink onto the light color pen.

You have to work quickly, before the ink dries. Look closely at the stamp before you press it onto the paper. Areas that glisten are still moist, while dull places have begun to dry. To re-moisten the ink, breathe on it with an open-mouthed "hah" just before stamping. Another way to keep the ink wet is to give it a light spritz of water from a plant mister.

New brush markers can be very wet, and if you use a spritzer, you might lose control of the moisture. If you think there's too much ink on the paper, simply turn it over and blot it lightly on a piece of clean newsprint.

Use the translucent nature of dye inks to blend one color into another. To create a third color that is a blend of two colors, ink over the part of the stamp that has the darker color on it with a lighter color pen, pulling some of the darker ink into the lighter area. Stamp while the ink is still wet. You'll see the third color appear in the zone between the original two colors. Be sure to clean the dark ink off your lighter brush marker by holding it on your cleaning plate.

While dye inks can be used to create many beautiful effects, the colors might not be light-fast. If you leave your artwork in bright sunlight, you have to expect the colors to fade.

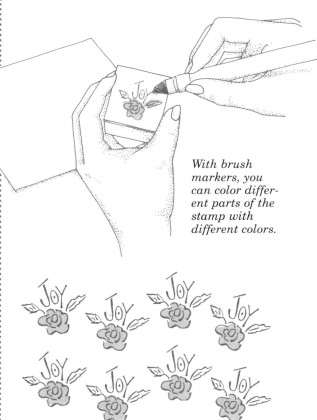

With brush markers, you can color different parts of the stamp with different colors.

INKING WITH PIGMENT INKS

*P*igment ink is a kind of paint dissolved in water. Unlike dye-based ink, it's opaque. This means that you cannot stamp one color over another, and also the color of the paper will not affect the color of the ink.

*P*igment ink comes in pads of many different colors and shapes, including metallic shades like gold, silver, bronze, and copper. Unlike dye ink, pigment ink resists fading in the light. It also has a balanced pH, which makes it unlikely to react with residual chemicals found in some papers. This is why pigment ink is ideal for use with photos and other artwork, as when creating scrapbooks or memory books.

*T*he best way to ink a stamp with pigment ink is with the image facing upward. With this method you can cover the largest stamp with a small ink pad. Gently tap the entire image with the ink pad, then hold the stamp at an angle in the light to look for dry spots. Tap those areas that need inking with the ink pad again, but be careful not to apply too much ink. If you do, the ink is liable to clog some parts of the design, making it difficult to stamp a clear image. Try removing excess ink by stamping gently on scrap paper before stamping your good artwork. You might have to use your cleaning plate to remove the excess ink. If you're not sure that the surface of the stamp has been covered evenly, it's best to remove all of the ink and start over.

*B*ecause pigment ink dries slowly, it works best on absorbent papers. To use it on

When using small pads of pigment ink, it's best to tap the stamp with the ink pad.

glossy coated papers, you have to emboss it to make it permanent. Because the ink dries slowly, sprinkled embossing powder will cling to it. When you heat the paper, the embossing powder fuses with the ink to create a lustrous raised image. There's more about embossing on page 57.

INKING WITH RAINBOW PADS

*R*ainbow ink pads, which contain more than one color of ink, are an easy way to add variety to stamped art. Some rainbow pads contain three or more different colors, while others contain several shades of the same color.

*R*ainbow pads are available with both dye inks and pigment inks. Sooner or later, the colors in a dye ink pad will run together, creating new colors where they blend. You can slow this process by cleaning your stamp after each impression, and by always storing the pad flat. The colors in a pigment ink pad tend not to blend together, though you might contaminate one color with another by

transferring ink with your stamp. When this happens, restore the original color simply by wiping the pad surface with a clean paper towel.

*S*ome rainbow pads have plastic dividers or some other mechanical device to keep the colors apart between uses. The space for the divider might leave an un-inked line on your stamp. Compensate for this by moving the stamp a little bit as you tap it on the pad.

*D*ye rainbow pads will produce dazzling results, especially on gloss-coated paper. If you have a brayer, try using it with a rainbow pad to create a terrific background.

OTHER KINDS OF INK

*A*lmost any water-soluble ink or paint will work with your rubber stamps. Poster paint and acrylic paint both work well. However, be sure to clean your stamp thoroughly after each ink you try. And avoid office ink pads, because they might contain chemicals that will dry out and damage the rubber in your stamps.

For an interesting effect try stamping an image on dark-colored paper using ordinary household bleach instead of ink. You'll be able to watch the faded negative image appear. The shades of color depend mostly on the nature of the dyes used to color the paper, so you have to experiment. Don't reach conclusions until the bleach dries, because it will continue to work on the colors as long as there's any moisture present.

Planning Your Project

The success of your project depends upon how well you choose your inks, pencils, markers, paper, and colors. Be sure to experiment with the materials available to you, to see which ones work best together. Once you gain a little experience, you'll become able to imagine how your artwork might look, and how to use your kit of materials and techniques to create the messages you want to send.

The nice thing about rubber-stamp images is, if you don't like the effect, try something else. Try a different color, another paper, a new layout. You can also add hand-drawn elements to your designs. If you keep them simple, you won't have to worry about the level of your drawing ability—and if you make a mistake, it's easy to start over.

For example, suppose you have stamped a bouquet of flowers. You can add the suggestion of leaves with a few strokes of a green marker, or a new spray of flowers with a few scattered dots. To add a new flower to the bouquet, simply use your brush markers to ink a single blossom in the bouquet that's on the stamp.

Don't worry that you have to come up with every idea on your own. Visit a card shop and browse the greetings on display. Go to the library and borrow some books on crafts and graphic arts. It's OK to copy a copyrighted image, as long as you aren't planning to sell it to someone else. When you do find an element you like, you'll be combining it with your own touches, so your personality and approach will always shine through.

LEARNING ABOUT PAPERS

There are thousands of kinds of paper, and most of them can be used for rubber stamping. You'll find plain white papers, colored papers, and printed pattern papers in a wide variety of textures and weights. You can also find marbled, metallic, and glitter papers, as well as handmade papers with many interesting surface textures. However, when you shop for papers be aware that some grades are extremely expensive, and don't buy more than you're sure you'll be able to use. The salespeople at stores that sell art supplies and rubber stamps usually know a lot about papers, and are delighted to help you learn more.

*B*esides the samples of paper in your kit, try working on tissue paper, drawing paper, and lightweight card stock. In general, text-weight papers will be most suitable for layering, letter-writing, and making envelopes. Cover paper or index paper is more suitable for making cards, gift tags, boxes, and other sturdy projects. A good place to start is with uncoated white card stock, like the cards enclosed in the kit. It's stiff enough to be easy to use, it accepts all kind of ink, and it's inexpensive so you don't have to worry about waste.

*G*lossy or coated papers will produce the brightest colors from dye-based inks and markers. Glossy paper might be a little slippery, so be sure to hold it down and still when you lift the stamp, so you don't accidentally smear the image. Pigment inks require matte paper, because it will absorb the moisture from the ink and allow it to dry. Watch out for "matte-coated" papers, which may be called "matte." They won't hold pigment ink unless you also emboss the image.

*T*he technique of cutting, tearing, and gluing pieces of paper together to create images is called "collage." It's a terrific way to add dimension to your projects. Try layering different papers, and tearing the paper around images you have stamped. The way to do this without tearing into the image itself is to hold the image area firmly down on the worktable with one hand, while you tear away the surrounding paper with the other or, simply tear the paper to the shape you want before stamping on it.

*T*ry tearing in different directions, and with the back side of the image facing down instead of up. You'll find that tearing one way produces a flat edge, while tearing the other way leaves a layered edge. Try inking both kinds of edge with a brush marker. You'll notice that the layered edge absorbs the ink and becomes darker, while the flat edge does not. Use these different effects in assembling your collage.

To tear a reasonably straight edge, use a ruler as a guide. You can even buy rulers with an uneven (or deckled) edge that are made for tearing paper. You can also cut the paper with decorative-edged scissors like those included with this kit. Some papers tear better, and leave a prettier edge, if you wet them first. Use a small paintbrush dipped in water to wet the line you wish to tear, and see what happens.

Tissue paper is light and somewhat transparent, which makes it perfect for special-effect overlays, and it comes in dozens of colors. It's also inexpensive, so you can experiment as much as you like with it. Because it's transparent, a stamped design will show from both sides. And because it's so light, gluing it to heavier material creates a very interesting surface. However, when you stamp it the ink will tend to bleed through, so be sure to protect your work surface with newsprint.

Another interesting paper is adhesive-backed (sometimes called sticker paper, or "crack-and-peel" paper). You can stamp an image on it, then cut out the image, peel the backing off, and stick it onto your artwork. Use adhesive-backed paper to make such gifts as bookplates, jar labels, and stickers.

Some papers come in rolls, making them suitable for gift wrapping. Try white or brown Kraft paper, poster paper, or uncoated shelf paper. You can even use 11 x 17 copy-machine paper to make book covers and wrapping paper for small gifts, and you can make a decorative ribbon by stamping on rolls of adding-machine tape. Be sure to test before you buy a lot of anything, however—some gift-wrapping paper has a coating that may make stamping difficult or impossible.

Your mailbox can be an excellent source of interesting papers for collage. Tear colorful images out of magazines, advertisements, and junk mail. You may find that some magazines and circulars are printed on unusual paper, with enough blank areas for stamping. Printed papers can be ideal for making a decorative background or a cut-out frame, and to line envelopes or boxes. Postage stamps, both new and cancelled, make wonderful additions to collage cards, as do some kinds of candy wrappers. Working with paper that you would otherwise discard is not only challenging and fun, it's also a good way to recycle.

LAYOUT AND DESIGN

*G*ood designs don't happen by themselves. Someone created them. And while there are no firm rules for good design, there are some things to pay attention to. What's most important is learning how to hear the little voice within you that tells you when something looks right. You might not be able to say why it looks so good, but that doesn't matter. What does matter is that you cultivate your own sense of what looks right, and learn how to trust your own eye. When some part of a design doesn't look right to you, work on it some more. And when you think something looks just perfect, chances are others will agree.

*D*esigning your project is probably the most exciting part of creating it. All the possibilities are wide open, and you can take your idea wherever you like. This is when you decide what you want your artwork to say, and how it will communicate that message to other people. Your message might be a simple statement of beauty, made with interesting colors and pretty shapes—and it doesn't have to be any more complicated than that. But it might also be something heartfelt and spiritually meaningful. By giving your message whatever direction you like, you will make it your own unique expression.

COLOR

*W*hat do you want the recipient of your inspirational greeting to feel? Color has a lot to do with feelings. People like bright colors because they are cheerful, while pastels can be soft and soothing, and dark colors dignified, even somber. Color combinations that work together will feel harmonious, while discordant colors can make you feel jumpy, even irritated.

*W*hat makes some colors work well together, while other colors jump apart? One way to achieve color harmony is to

stay with closely related colors—shades and tints of the same basic hue, for example. In another approach to color harmony, you try to connect any two colors through a third color that contains them both. For example, red and blue can be linked through purple, which is made by mixing red and blue. Similarly, blue and yellow connect through green, while red and yellow combine to make orange. There are many other ways to make colors work together, and most art handbooks will help you get started. As with the overall design, however, the key is learning how to trust your own eye. If a certain combination of colors gives you a feeling you like, chances are other people will respond in the same way.

COMPOSITION

The term "composition" means how you place images on a card or project, and how they relate to the overall shape of the card. Composition has the same kind of effect on people as color. A composition can be exciting or unpredictable, soothing and predictable, disconcerting, or just plain boring. By being aware of basic

design concepts, you can affect how people respond to your work.

Let's begin with the shape of your card. A square card is the same size in length and in width. A square is a simple shape, some people might think too simple. The square is so symmetrical that it practically forces you to center your stamped images on it. A good exercise is to cut some squares of paper, choose a stamp you like, and print the image in different places on the squares. See whether you prefer centered images, or off-center images. There is no "correct" answer. It depends on what you like, and on the message you wish to send.

It's hard to go wrong with a centered design.

Most cards are rectangular, with one side longer than the other. A square is the same whichever way is up, but a rectangle can have its long side vertical, or horizontal. Some people use the word "portrait" to describe a card that's standing up vertically, and "landscape" to describe one that's horizontal.

Images placed off-center create an interesting look.

A card with a "portrait" orientation gives you several ways to place the imagery.

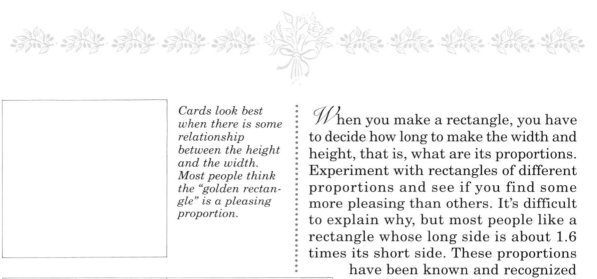

When you make a rectangle, you have to decide how long to make the width and height, that is, what are its proportions. Experiment with rectangles of different proportions and see if you find some more pleasing than others. It's difficult to explain why, but most people like a rectangle whose long side is about 1.6 times its short side. These proportions have been known and recognized since Biblical times. Sometimes a rectangle with these proportions is called a "golden rectangle."

Take a look at paintings you like, and see whether their focal point is on center or somewhere off center. You'll soon find examples of both. A famous example is *The Last Supper* by Leonardo da Vinci. This large painting is almost exactly twice as wide as it is high, and the face of Jesus—the focal point—is positioned in the exact center of the rectangle.

An interesting way to plan a stamping layout is to divide the space into thirds both ways, like a tic-tac-toe board. This makes nine boxes. Now try placing your

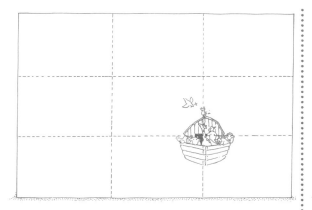

Divide the card in thirds both ways, then lay out your images where the lines intersect.

Dividing the card into a grid helps you place strong visual elements. The blank spaces are as important as the stamped ones.

stamped images in different ways relative to the boxes. You'll probably find that the most dynamic locations are where the lines intersect, so try arranging your design around one of those places. Try to resist the urge to fill the whole card with imagery—a blank space is as important as a stamped space.

When you create a scene using different sized stamps, remember that objects closer to the eye appear larger, while objects farther away appear smaller. Use your small stamps to make background images, and your large ones for fore-

ground images. Layering the images on different pieces of paper will create a very realistic illusion of depth. But you don't have to do it this way, you can combine images in any way you like, whether or not the effect is realistic.

Always plan your layouts on scrap paper before you commit your good materials. A good way to experiment with composition is to stamp your images on scrap paper, then cut them out. Use the cut-outs to try different arrangements. Try many different versions before you settle on the one you like best. One of the

nicest things about rubber stamping is that you never have to do the same thing twice. Even when you are making a series of cards for a single occasion, you don't have to make them all exactly the same. In fact these small variations are what most people like best about hand-made artwork.

STAMP AND REPEAT

*Y*ou will get a lot of mileage out of a single stamp when you use it to make borders, patterns, and clusters. To make a simple border, use one color ink and stamp evenly across the bottom of a card, or all around the edges. For a different effect, try alternating colors, and instead of making all the images the same distance apart, try varying the spacing. To make a background pattern, stamp the same image all over your card. If you space the images evenly but change the angle of the stamp, you won't have to worry about perfect alignment.

*B*orders look best when all the elements are about the same size. When you

A small repeated image creates a pleasing feeling of rhythm and movement.

Changing the angle of the background stamp means you don't have to worry about precise placement.

The small images make a border that balances nicely with the large image in the center.

When the border images are too close to the size of the central motif, the image looks haphazard and out of balance.

make a border around a central image, the central image should be significantly larger than the border stamps. If the images were about the same size, the effect could be cluttered, or confusing.

*W*hen you want the stamped images to line up, use a ruler, a stamp positioner, or a strip of stiff cardboard as a guide. A guide that's thick enough to contact the stamp mount works best. When you want a row of equally spaced images, begin by stamping the center and both ends, then fill in the remaining spaces. For an interesting variation, stamp the center image, then vary the spacing as you work to the right and left of center. Try making the images closer together near the center and farther apart near the ends of the row. Then try it the other way around, with the center images farther apart than the outside ones.

*W*rapping paper can be charming when it's covered with stamped images that don't line up evenly. But you might prefer the precision of near-perfect spacing. One way to do this is to work over a grid drawn on white paper or foam core board. The advantage of a paper grid is that

To align the images on a page, place the stamp along the edge of a ruler or piece of cardboard.

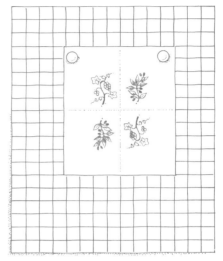

Placing your artwork on grid paper can help you align the images.

when you place it on a lightbox, if you have one, you will be able to see the marks through your good paper. The advantage of foam core is that you can thumbtack your good paper in position on it. If the foam core is larger than the good paper, you'll be able to space your images by eye, using the grid lines as a guide.

*H*ere's a tip for making wrapping paper. Before you begin to stamp, loosely wrap the gift in a piece of paper, then unwrap

it and flatten to stamp. This helps you figure out the most effective way to place the images, and it also avoids stamping paper you wouldn't be using.

*M*ultiple images can help create illusions of motion and depth. One way to create the feeling of motion is to stamp the foreground image first, then without re-inking, stamp shadow-images that recede in the direction you imagine the motion to be coming from. An all-over background will seem to have depth when you stamp a foreground image and (again without re-inking) several background images around it. Repeat similar clusters of strong and faint images all over the paper.

LAYERING

$\mathcal{O}$ne of the easiest and most effective ways to add interest and dimension to your stamped projects is to layer successively smaller pieces of paper or cardboard. This will create intriguing borders and is also a way to highlight the main idea of your project. Notice how many of the projects included in this book use this elegant technique.

MASKS

$\mathcal{M}$asks allow you to stamp one image so it overlaps another. This helps when you want to create a scene with one image appearing in front of another. Once you understand the basic technique of masking, you'll find many different ways to use it.

$\mathcal{B}$egin by stamping the image that is to appear in the foreground, that is, closest to the viewer. In our example, it's the rocks in front of the lighthouse.

$\mathcal{N}$ext, stamp the same image on a sticky note (a Post-it, for example) or on a piece of lightweight paper. Make sure the portion of the image where you want the

Step 1. Stamp the rocks on your card.

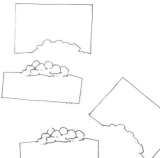

Step 2. Stamp the same image on two Post-its or two paper scraps, then cut them out to create masks.

Step 3. Stick one mask on top of the rocks you stamped in Step 1.

Step 4. Stamp the rocks on the card. Allow them to overlap onto the mask.

Step 5. Repeat step 4, using the other mask, and stamp on the card overlapping the two masks.

Step 6. Peel off the mask, leaving a perfect group of rocks as the base of the lighthouse.

overlap to occur is over the sticky part. Now use scissors or an X-Acto knife to cut the sticky note along the line of the overlap; in this example, along the top of the rocks. This is the mask, which you use to protect the image you already stamped.

*P*lace the mask on top of the good image. Now stamp the second image, the one you want to appear "behind" the first one. The mask allows you to overlap the images as much as you like.

*S*ometimes the thickness of the mask might interfere with the stamp, and you may have to press extra hard to get

a clean image. When you remove the mask, the two images should butt perfectly together. In the example shown on these pages, the lighthouse will look like it is sitting on top of a large pile of rocks.

*T*he same mask can be used as many times as you like, and it's easy to make a new mask for each new situation. This technique is especially useful when you want to make an edition of greeting cards using the same combination of stamps. Store the masks you wish to keep in individual envelopes. Mark the outside of each envelope with the image and mask contained within.

$\mathcal{A}$ mask can help you control where the ink goes, and does not go, on a card. Remember that folded cards should always be flattened before stamping, so the fold doesn't interfere with getting a clear image. That's fine, until you want to stamp right up to the fold without getting ink on the back side. If you cover the back side with a paper mask, you'll solve the problem. Stamp the image, then remove the mask to reveal a straight, clean edge at the fold.

FRAMES

$\mathcal{A}$ttractive borders and frames set off your design. Small stamps repeated many times are especially useful for creating borders and frames. Remember that the frame can be made by stamping around an image, or it can be created by leaving the card itself blank around the edges. Another way to make a frame is to draw marker lines around the card. Try coloring the card's edge with the face of the brush marker. This can make an especially attractive border on a torn or deckled edge.

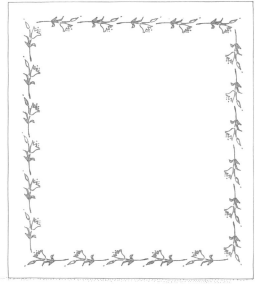

A repeated pattern creates an attractive frame. A small image works best.

$\mathcal{A}$n easy way to lay out a frame is by lightly drawing the shape you want. Then stamp all along the penciled line with a small design you like. Let the ink dry thoroughly before you erase any visible pencil lines. Or, you may want to include the pencil lines as part of your design.

$\mathcal{Y}$ou don't have to stamp every inch of a frame. It will look fine if you only stamp

Four corner images can also define a frame. Connect the corners with a marker line.

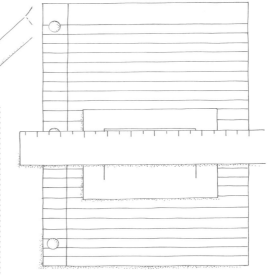

Placing your artwork on a piece of ruled paper helps you draw parallel lines.

the four corners. This kind of virtual frame can be solidified by drawing lines or dots to connect the corner images.

*A*n easy tool for drawing parallel lines is a regular lined notebook. Position your card in the middle of the page, with its top edge on one of the ruled lines. Now connect the lines across the card with a ruler. Rotate the card to draw the complete frame.

TEMPLATES

A mask with a hole in it is called a mortise mask, or a template. You can use one to make a wonderfully clean-edged design. Draw the shape you want on a piece of copier paper and cut it out. Work on a piece of mat board, or if you have one, on a plastic mat made for cutting. Cut straight-edged designs with a sharp

X-Acto knife pulled along a metal-edged ruler. Press the ruler down with one hand, and pull the knife with the other; always pull the knife away from your holding hand, never toward it. If the shape you want is curved, try cutting it freehand with the X-Acto knife. To cut perfect circles, fit an X-Acto knife into a school compass. Make sure the knife blade follows the circle, and doesn't turn sideways in the compass.

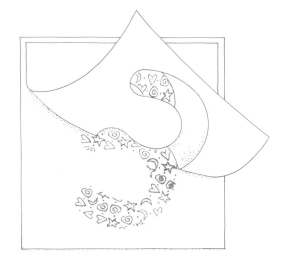

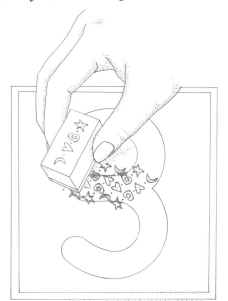

A paper template, or mortise mask, helps you stamp within clean-edged shapes.

When you finish stamping, remove the mask to reveal your mask shape.

Place the new template on your card stock and stamp many small images into the opening—the "live area." Let some of them overlap the mask. When you remove it, you'll enjoy a marvelously clean-edged, framed design.

The cut-out part also can be used as a mask when you wish to stamp the background. First stamp the main image through the mortise mask. Then remove the mortise mask, cover the stamped shape with the mask, and stamp the background around the cut-out piece.

These techniques will help you to produce large, bold designs with small stamps. In addition, you can add an interesting frame by masking off the center of a card and then stamping around the mask.

THE STAMP POSITIONER

The stamp positioner helps you place a stamped image precisely where you want it. It's possible to be precise enough to stamp one image exactly over another. This technique can save a project containing images that, for whatever reason, aren't stamped as clearly as you'd like.

The stamp positioner is an L-shaped or T-shaped piece of clear Lucite, or it can be a wooden bracket, thick enough to contact the stamp mount and not the rubber die. It is used with a piece of tracing paper, as follows:

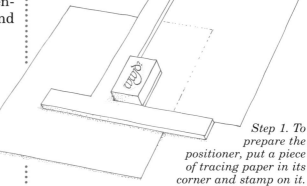

Step 1. To prepare the positioner, put a piece of tracing paper in its corner and stamp on it.

Step 2. Use the stamped tracing paper to properly place the positioner before restamping.

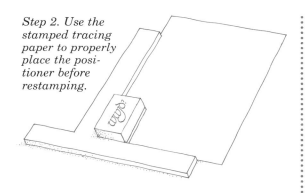

Step 3. Remove the tracing paper and stamp the artwork.

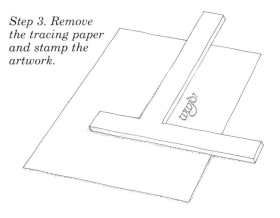

To begin, color the right-angled edges of the tracing paper with a marker. The color helps you see that the paper neatly contacts the positioner, and hasn't slipped underneath it.

Fit the paper into the positioner and stamp the image onto it. Slide the stamp along the two sides of the positioner before you press it onto the paper. Now move the tracing paper around on your artwork to see where you want to stamp it. Hold the tracing paper in the right place, bring the positioner up to its colored edges, remove the paper, and stamp.

Follow the same sequence when you have to re-stamp an image. Stamp the tracing paper using the positioner, then lay it over the defective image. Fiddle the paper into the exact right place so you can bring the positioner up snug, then remove the tracing paper and re-stamp.

Re-stamping can enhance an outline image and give it depth. Stamp the image in the lighter color, color it in with markers or pencils, then re-stamp it with the darker color. The second image also can be embossed (see page 57).

Instead of tracing paper, you can use a thin sheet of clear Lucite, which is re-usable. Clean the Lucite on your cleaning plate, or with water and a paper towel.

CREATING
BACKGROUNDS

There are many ways to create a background for your stamped artwork. Start with paper that is the color and finish you like, then give it texture and richness by spattering, by sponging, or by using a brayer, which is a small rubber roller like a trim roller for paint. Once you begin to experiment you'll be able to create many interesting background effects.

SPATTERING

You know how drawing your toothbrush over the edge of the water glass makes a spatter. You can use this same effect to spray millions of tiny ink dots onto your artwork. Make a background with the spattered ink, or else spatter through a mask or stencil to color the main subject.

Any water-soluble stamping ink can be spattered, but acrylic paint works very well too. Mix the ink with water in a disposable cup or a small can, then dip an old toothbrush into it. Hold the toothbrush bristles down above the paper, then scrape the bristles over a stick or pencil. More paint makes bigger spatters, while a brush that's nearly dry makes tiny dots. For the most control, work with a dryer brush (tap it on scrap paper to dump excess ink), then spatter again to build up the pattern you want.

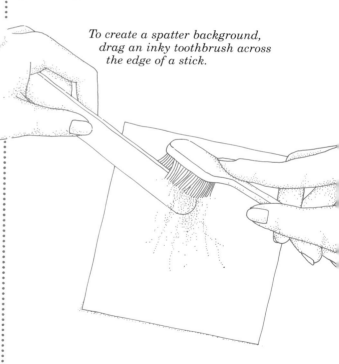

To create a spatter background, drag an inky toothbrush across the edge of a stick.

SPONGING

*I*f you apply stamping ink to a sponge, it can be used to place soft clouds of color on the paper. There are many different kinds of sponges, and each will make a different effect. Try cosmetic sponges, household sponges, and natural sponges. Each works well. You might even find art sponges that have been designed to make background effects. A very fine sponge, like a cosmetic sponge, will make an air-brushed effect, the household sponge creates mottling, while a coarse bath sponge leaves a lacy image.

*T*o get started with sponges, try coloring a dry household sponge with a water-based marker. Remove any excess ink by blotting the sponge on scrap paper. Now lightly tap it all over your good paper. Some sponges will make many images before they need to be re-inked, while others will only make one or two. You have to experiment to see how each sponge behaves. Also, try applying color by tapping the sponge onto an ink pad.

*T*here are a number of ways to vary the effects you get from sponges. If your sponge has square corners, try making it into a rounded pillow by gathering its edges between your fingertips. If your sponge is round and you'd like it to print a square edge, try cutting it with scissors. It's convenient to work with several sponges at a time, one for each color. When you're done with a project, clean your sponges by squishing soapy water through them, followed by a thorough rinse in running water.

*Y*ou'll also want to experiment with different inks. Sponges allow you to mix colors right on the paper. For example, you could build a landscape by sponging misty hillsides in green, brown, and

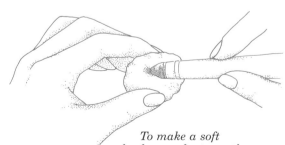

To make a soft background, stamp the paper with a sponge that has been inked with a brush marker.

purple against a hazy blue sky. For subtle effects, try transparent dye inks on colored paper. Try working with ink that's almost the same color as the paper, as well as with contrasting colors, and see which effect you like best. Pigment inks aren't transparent, so the color of the paper won't show through. This produces quite a different look.

For a dazzling effect, try sponging metallic inks or paints onto your background. To control the shape of the image, try sponging over the edge of a stencil or mask. See what happens if you move the mask, then sponge the paper again. When you find a mask you like and want to use again, cut it out of a sheet of clear acrylic acetate. Then you will be able to wipe it clean to re-use it with different colors.

You aren't restricted to textures produced by the sponge itself, either. Try sponging over a piece of lace fabric, or a paper doily, a piece of netting, or a wire screen. Also try sponging techniques using other materials, like wadded-up tissue paper, paper towels, or facial tissue. Each material will produce a different effect. Scrunch up the sponging material in your fingers, ink it, and tap it lightly on your artwork.

Sponging over a template makes a background with a shaped opening. This helps you build scenes.

THE BRAYER

When you want to lay down a smooth background color, use a rubber brayer.

It's the small paint roller that print makers use to apply ink to linoleum blocks and other kinds of printing plates. Not only can you use a brayer to ink your stamps, but it's also great for rolling background inks directly onto the paper.

Brayers come in many widths. They can be used with any kind of water-soluble ink, or with acrylic paint. Pigment inks work best on uncoated paper, while dye-based inks work best on coated paper.

Set up your work area by spreading a large sheet of newsprint under your good paper. You will want to roll the brayer off the edge of the paper without making a mess. Use a regular stamp pad to ink your brayer, or a rainbow pad, or pour the ink or paint into a small, flat pan.

To load the brayer with ink, roll it firmly over the pad or into the color in the pan. Roll the brayer back and forth in the ink so it covers the whole surface evenly. Now roll the ink onto your good paper or card. Land the brayer a finger's width onto the newsprint, then roll onto your artwork. Roll in one direction, and lift the brayer between strokes. Clean the brayer between colors by rolling any remain-

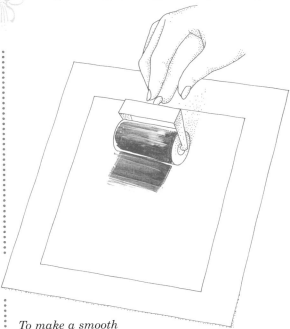

To make a smooth background, roll ink onto the paper with a brayer.

ing ink onto the newsprint. Then roll across your cleaning pad and wipe on a paper towel.

BRAYER TECHNIQUES

By brayering, you can make colored paper in all your ink colors. Then stamp, paint, or draw your messages and greetings on the brayer-colored paper. Another fascinating way to create images is to block some of the brayered ink from reaching the paper. You can cut masks of paper, plastic, or tape. Masking liquids, such as rubber cement, are called resists.

*L*ike photographic film, paper masks can be positive or negative. For example, cut a circle out of a piece of paper, then use the paper around the hole (mortise mask) to mask everything but the circular opening. Or, use the paper circle itself as the mask while you brayer ink across the rest of your card. Cover-up tape, which comes in several widths, is another kind of mask. Try brayering ink over a taped pattern, then when the ink dries, rearrange the tape and brayer another color of ink. This is a good way to make plaid.

*T*o try a very simple resist technique, make a drawing with ordinary wax crayons and then brayer the ink over it. Since wax repels water, the crayoned areas will repel your water-soluble inks. Crayons can make a lovely effect like batik cloth, with soft lines and mottled areas. For designs with firmer edges, try painting the image with rubber cement or a printmaker's liquid masking material. Brayer the ink over the design, then rub the resist off the paper with your fingers, or with a rubber-cement pickup eraser.

*F*or an unusual resist effect, stamp an image with clear embossing ink, and emboss it with clear embossing powder. (To learn about embossing, see page 57). When you roll colored ink over the image, the embossing materials will resist it, so the underlying paper color shows through. If any stray color sticks to the embossed area, wipe it off with a cotton cloth or a paper towel.

*A*nother novel way of laying down a background pattern is to draw it directly on the brayer, using regular water-based markers. Specially designed roller stamps have raised images repeated around the roller.

*P*rint makers like to use a piece of plate glass to roll out their inks. If you have ink in bottles or tubes, try squeezing a few drops directly onto the glass. Load the brayer by rolling it through the ink. To create rainbow effects and marbled patterns, use several different inks at a time.

ADDING COLOR AND SPARKLE

There are many ways to add color and sparkle to your stamped greetings. You can color your messages with colored pencils, markers, chalks, watercolor paints, watercolor pencils, and acrylics. You can make your greetings sparkle with glitter and glitter-filled glue.

COLORED PENCILS AND MARKERS

Many stamped images consist of an outline, with no large filled-in areas. Such stamps are said to be "open." Color them like a coloring book, using pencils or markers. Stamp the outline image with a dark ink, wait for the ink to dry, then color away.

Color always makes a stunning difference in images of this type, with fine-tip markers delivering bright, intense colors, and colored pencils imparting a softer feeling. However, you must take care to match the type of paper to your colors: pencils don't stick to glossy paper, while markers may bleed on matte paper.

When you want to achieve subtle gradations of color, use colored pencils. The harder you press, the more intense the color. Pencil colors also can be layered, to create depth and shadows. Colored pencil often looks best against a soft outline, which you can create by stamping first on scrap paper to discharge the extra ink, before stamping a second time on good paper.

WATERCOLOR

Watercolor can be beautiful with rubber-stamped images, and there are many ways to give your greetings the look of a watercolor painting. However, since most stamp ink is water soluble, painting over an image probably will make it run. You can prevent this by stamping with permanent ink, or by embossing the ink after stamping. (To learn about embossing, see page 57.)

Watercolor paint comes in tubes and in paintboxes containing little squares of solidified pigment. Pick it up and apply it with the moistened tip of a small, fine, flexible brush. You don't need an expensive brush, so long as it's flexible and comes to a neat point when wet. Watercolor is an excellent medium when you want to color in an image, and also when you want to paint a shadow alongside it. Water makes the colors appear soft and diffuse.

*W*hile watercolor paints can be quite difficult to use, watercolor pencils are easy. When they're dry, they work like any other colored pencil. When you add water with a small brush, the colors run and flow like paint.

*A*n interesting way to use watercolor pencils is first to color the stamped image, then blend the colors with a clean, moistened brush. Try misting the image with water from a spray bottle before you tackle it with the brush.

*H*ow you manage the water affects the intensity of watercolor pencils. To create strong colors, wet the paper first, then draw with dry pencils. Be sure to use heavy watercolor paper, because regular drawing paper has no strength when wet. For the most intense col-

ors, dip the pencil in water, then draw on either wet or dry paper.

*Y*ou can use watercolor pencils just as if they were a paintbox of colors. Take pigment off the tip of the pencil with a moistened brush, then paint your stamped image with it. To mix colors, blend them together with a wet brush on a separate piece of watercolor paper. Then pick up the blended color on the brush and paint with it.

To blend the colors in an image, brush over them with a small amount of water.

The ink in brush markers is similar to watercolor paint. When you want light and subtle colors, try coloring your markers onto a plastic palette or aluminum foil, then pick up the color with a wet brush. Use brush-point blenders to help you blend ink from brush markers.

Water may make your paper curl, but it will flatten out again as it dries. If it doesn't, press it flat between heavy books overnight. You can probably get the same effects with less water.

CHALKS

Colored chalks, or pastels, come in the form of round crayons or square sticks. They create soft, light, almost luminous colors, and they can be used on almost any kind of paper. Chalked images are extremely fragile and easy to smudge, but they can be made permanent by spraying with a workable fixative. "Workable" means that you can fix a drawing, and then continue to work on it with your chalks.

For an unusual effect, stamp on glossy black paper, then emboss the images with white embossing powder and color them with chalk or pastel. Remove excess chalk from the paper with a damp sponge.

GLITTER

Glitter always adds sparkle and excitement to a message. You can't stamp with glitter ink, but you can add glitter to a stamped project with glitter glue. It comes in plastic squeeze bottles and in pens with many different size tips. The glue itself is transparent and dries invisibly, leaving the glitter behind. It's excellent for making sparkly little accents, and also for filling in or outlining stamped images. A glittery outline on two adjacent sides of an image will even add an illusion of depth.

$\mathcal{T}$o use glitter glue, dab lightly on the spot you'd like to highlight, or gently squeeze the bottle as you drag its tip across your paper. If it's not bright enough, sprinkle it with dry glitter of the same or another color while the glue is still wet. For extra control, apply the glue and the glitter separately. The glue will dry in 2 to 4 hours.

$\mathcal{G}$lue will ruin a rubber stamp, so never put it directly on the rubber die. Even though the application of glitter should be the last step in a project, you proba-bly will end up getting some glitter on a stamp. Remove it with the sticky side of a loop of tape.

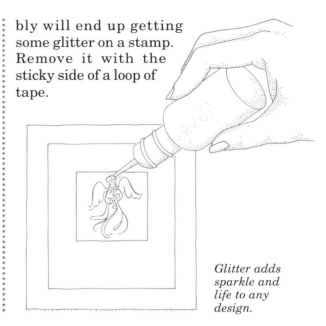

Glitter adds sparkle and life to any design.

EMBOSSING

*E*mbossing transforms an ordinary stamped image into one with depth and the luster of metal or glass. Embossing is a professional technique that's easy and fun to do. Traditionally, embossing meant raising a design by pressing paper onto a metal die. You can't do that with a rubber stamp, but you can achieve the same effect with special heat-set embossing inks and powders.

*B*efore the ink dries, dust the stamped image with embossing powder. When you heat the powder, it melts and fuses.

*B*esides their beauty and impact, embossed images have another advantage: the heat-set material is durable and no longer water soluble. Embossed images don't fade in the light. Better yet, embossing works on any kind of paper and many other surfaces, including wood and terra-cotta.

INKS AND POWDERS FOR EMBOSSING

*P*igment inks work best for embossing, because they dry slowly. Dye inks may dry before you can sprinkle them with embossing powder. You can also stamp and draw with embossing fluid, which comes in a pad or dauber-topped bottle. Clear or colored embossing pens also come with fine, calligraphic, and brush tips.

*T*here are many different kinds of embossing powder, with new ones being introduced all the time. Start with clear embossing powder, which works with the color of the ink. For different effects, try lustrous metallic powders, colored powders, and sparkly tinsel powders. Pearlescent and iridescent powders will catch and refract the light, and texture powders will give your artwork the look and feel of such textured materials as pottery or cement.

*Y*ou can even get embossing powders that are formulated for different kinds of stamped images. For stamps with fine lines, try detail powder. It can pick up very fine lines in the stamped design, with the trade-off of not raising the design as high as other powders. For bold stamps with broad areas of color, try extra-thick embossing powder, which also can be used for double embossing.

Along with embossing powders, you will need a 300-degree Fahrenheit (150 degrees Centigrade) heat source. Stamp shops sell an efficient heat gun. Although the gun looks like a hair dryer, it reaches a higher temperature. A hair dryer will not work because it doesn't get hot enough. Other heat sources that will work include a toaster oven set to 300 degrees, or a regular electric iron set for cottons.

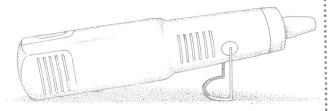

A heat gun fuses the embossing powder to your design.

HOW TO EMBOSS

Embossing is a simple process that is certain to amaze you the first time you try it. Just stamp or draw your image using pigment ink, embossing fluid, or ink from a brush-tip embossing pen. Before the ink has a chance to dry, sprinkle the entire image with embossing powder. Don't worry about using too much because you can't—the next step is to tilt the paper and tap it so the extra powder slides off. Catch it on a piece of scrap paper, which you can then bend into a funnel shape for pouring the powder back into its bottle.

Before you fire up the heat gun, take a look at the image. You'll see that the powder has adhered to the ink. It will glisten and sparkle in the light. Check to see whether the powder has stuck anywhere you don't want to emboss. If so, brush it off with a dry paintbrush, or with a clean cosmetic sponge. Don't brush it off with your fingers, because skin oils on the paper will make the powders on the paper stick where you don't want them.

To melt the embossing powder, hold the heat gun about 6 inches away and move it in slow circles. You will see the powder melt, rise, and fuse to the paper. As soon as you see the lines rise up, stop heating it. To do the same job with an electric iron, hold the paper over the iron and move it in circles. The powder will be set as soon as it cools. Wait for it to cool, then touch the image. You will feel how shiny and slick it has become.

Too much heat is liable to dull the colors and flatten the embossing, and it might also scorch the paper. Control the amount of heat by putting more or less distance between its source and your paper. You only need enough heat to melt the powder. Once you see it start to melt, take the heat away.

Heat can affect some papers, so it always pays to test before you emboss. Sometimes the heat will change the paper color, but don't panic—when it cools it might change right back again. The heat might also warp the paper. If so, flatten it under a heavy book for an hour or two, with a clean sheet to protect the image.

Once you decide that you like embossed greetings, you'll probably want to get set up for doing it regularly. If you don't have a heat gun, invest in one. It will be useful for other craft projects as well. Protect your fingers by using clothespins or toast tongs to hold cards while you heat them. We like to use sandwich-sized plastic containers with lids for storing embossing powders. They allow you to dip your images directly into the powder, and they make it easy to tip excess powder back into the container.

Sprinkle embossing powder on the stamped image before the ink has a chance to dry.

Tip the extra powder back into its container. Tap the card to remove all of the excess.

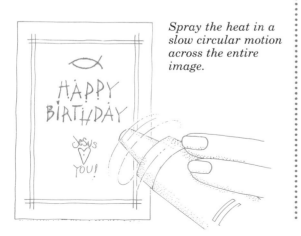

Spray the heat in a slow circular motion across the entire image.

EMBOSSING PENS AND GLUE STICKS

$\mathcal{T}$here are many special techniques to try with embossing powders. One of the most versatile tools is an embossing pen or brush-tip embossing marker. Use it to emboss parts of a previously stamped image, to repair mistakes, and to add borders or other drawings to your stamped images. However, when you want to emboss on or around a stamped image, be sure to wait for the stamp ink to dry completely. Otherwise you're likely to lose control of where the powder sticks and where it doesn't.

$\mathcal{G}$lue sticks and glue pens work well with embossing powders. Glue sticks come with many different kinds of tips, and they can be used like regular pens and brushes to draw borders, designs, and written greetings.

MULTIPLE EMBOSSING

*Y*ou don't have to emboss the entire image with one kind of powder. You can apply different powders to different parts of the image. Metallic powders like gold, silver, and copper can create spectacular effects. Start by inking the entire stamp with one shade of pigment ink or embossing fluid. Then sprinkle the powders on the various parts of the image, one at a time. Tap each powder off before you add the next, and don't apply any heat until the end. Then use the heat gun to fuse all the powders at once.

MAKING BORDERS

*E*mbossing powders will help you create many different kinds of borders. To make a narrow, artistic border, try dragging the edge of a card through pigment ink or embossing fluid. Then dip the edge in embossing powder and apply heat. This technique makes a border that flows right over the edge of the card. For a wider border, guide a chisel-point glue stick or embossing pen along the edge of the card. Like a deckled edge, this kind of border looks especially nice on the free edge of a folded card. It not only sets off your design, but also shows the recipient where to open the card.

*F*or fancy borders and frames, try using embossing pens. Some kinds of pens have ball points, while others have calligraphy tips and domed tips. Use them to draw lines, dots, dashes, and squiggles, using a ruler or working freehand. Some embossing pens are even erasable, so you can make a mistake and correct it.

A very elegant way to use embossing pens is to stamp a small image in each

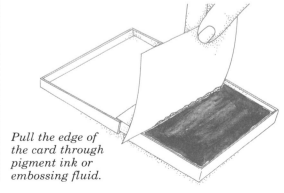

Pull the edge of the card through pigment ink or embossing fluid.

Run the glue stick along the edge of the card.

corner of your card, then connect the images. This technique allows you to frame the name on a place card, or the address on an envelope. Experiment with different color combinations. For a calm effect, make the embossed border in the same color as the lettering inside it. For a rich look, make it with metallic or pearlescent powder.

DOUBLE EMBOSSING

*D*ouble embossing looks like dazzling enameled or stained-glass. First you emboss the design in the usual way, using colored inks and powders, then emboss over all or part of it with clear fluid and clear powder. The clear coat adds extra depth and shine. If you like this effect, try it with clear, ultra-thick embossing powder.

*A*nother way to double emboss is to sprinkle clear powder while the image is still hot. Sprinkle the powder into the already embossed portions of the image, and continue to heat it until all the material flows together.

ADVANCED
TECHNIQUES

Now that you have learned the basic techniques of stamping, you're ready for more advanced techniques. In this section you will find out how to reverse your images, give them depth and shadows, create the illusion of motion, and make them into pop-ups and pop-outs. You'll also find it challenging and fun to stamp images on other materials besides paper, such as fabric, wood, and glass.

REVERSING

When you reverse a stamped image, it faces the opposite way and looks like a reflection of itself. The trick is to stamp the image onto an intermediate rubber surface, such as a large eraser, using pigment ink. Then, while the ink is still wet, press the eraser onto your paper. Press hard to make a good print. If you're intrigued by the design possibilities of reversed images, look for a flat rubber stamp made specifically for reversing.

The reverse image is almost always lighter than the original image. When you want to use both images side by side, make them the same density by stamping the intermediate surface first, then stamp the paper without re-inking. This way, both the regular image and the reverse image will be the second image off the pad.

Be sure to clean the eraser or flat stamp right after stamping. Clean it on your cleaning plate, or use a damp paper towel, the same as you would clean your regular stamps.

Step 1. To reverse an image, first stamp it onto an eraser or another flat rubber surface, using pigment ink.

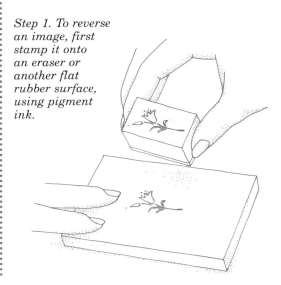

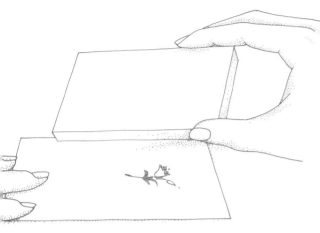

Step 2. Stamp the eraser or rubber surface onto your paper. Work quickly before the ink dries.

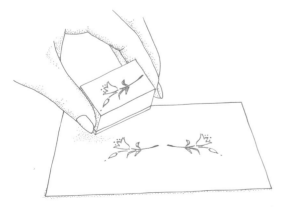

Step 3. Finally, stamp the artwork using the original stamp, without re-inking.

THE ILLUSION OF DEPTH

$\mathcal{S}$hadows create a natural illusion of depth. Normally the light comes from above and to one side, so the shadow falls below the image and along the side opposite the light source. To add a shadow to a stamped image, simply use markers to draw a line along the bottom edge and one side. Draw the shadow line with a light gray, blue, or lavender marker. When there is more than one image in your picture, make the shadow on the same side of each.

$\mathcal{A}$ very simple way to make an image lift off the card is to stamp it and cut part-way around it, using an X-Acto knife. Then bend the cut-out portion forward. This trick works best with simple, symmetrical images.

$\mathcal{A}$nother easy way to create an illusion of depth is to stamp the image in one color, then stamp it again nearby in a lighter color. For the most natural look, place the shadow image about 1/16-inch from the original, and off to one side.

For an even better depth illusion, cut a paper mask to keep the second image from interfering with the original. Make the mask by stamping the same image on a Post-it note, then cut it out with scissors. The weak Post-it glue sticks wherever you place it, then lifts away without marring the original image underneath. Stamp the new image over the mask and a little bit off to one side, then remove the mask. This trick makes a very realistic shadow, which fools the eye into believing the original image is floating above the paper.

These same techniques can make an image that really is lifted above the paper. First, stamp the image on your artwork. Second, stamp it again on another piece of the same paper or card. Cut out the second image, following the stamped outline. Now use glue and a scrap of thick card, or a piece of double-sided foam tape, to position the cut-out image over the top of the original stamped image. Try positioning the cut-out image exactly above the original, and also try shifting it a little bit. Position it a little bit upward and to the right or left. This makes the original image look like the shadow of the floating image.

Step 1. To make a three-dimensional image, stamp it on your artwork, then stamp it again on another piece of card.

Step 2. Cut out the second image.

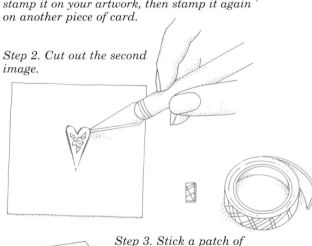

Step 3. Stick a patch of double-sided foam tape on the back of the cut-out image.

Step 4. The three-dimensional image looks as if it is rising off the card.

Three-dimensional cards are most successful when simpler images are used.

Create a sense of motion by stamping a series of images trailing away from the original.

THE ILLUSION OF MOTION

$\mathscr{T}$o make an image look like it is moving, stamp a trail of ghost images next to it. Begin by inking your stamp to make the "final" image in the series. Without re-inking, stamp the trailing images close together but running off in the direction from which you want the motion to begin. Varying the distance between images will make the motion speed up and slow down.

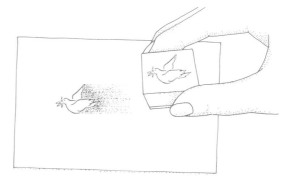

Another way to create motion is to drag the stamp across the paper.

POP-UPS AND POP-OUTS

*P*op-ups and pop-outs jump forward as you open the card. They work because there is a folded paper base or hinge that pushes the image out at you. The basic techniques are simple, but once you get the idea, you will be able to make startling scenes and illusions.

*B*egin by making the image that will pop up. It will be attached to a folded strip of card called the pop-up base. Stamp the image on its own piece of card, color it, and cut it out with scissors or an X-Acto knife.

*N*ext, make the pop-up base. Cut a strip of card stock 4 inches long and 1/2 inch wide. Fold the strip into four equal one-inch sections. Open your card flat and decide where along its foldline you want the pop-up image to be. As shown in the illustration, glue section 1 and section 4 to the two parts of the card, so their free ends meet at the fold. Gently close the card before the glue grabs, and adjust as necessary.

To make a pop-up base, fold a strip of paper into four sections. Glue sections 1 and 4 to your card.

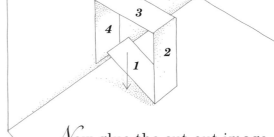

*N*ow glue the cut-out image onto section 2 of the pop-up base. Position the image carefully so it lies flat when you close the card. It will pop up automatically when you open the card.

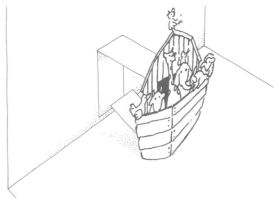

Glue the image onto section 2.

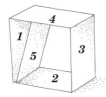

To make a pop-out base, fold a strip into five sections and glue it into a box shape.

Cut two slits across the fold of the inside card and tease the cut portion forward to create the platform, as shown in the illustration. Now stamp and draw your design on the inside of the card, and glue your pop-up image to the platform. Finally, glue the inside card to the second card, making sure to match their center folds. Press the two cards together flat before you gently close the card and test the pop-up action.

*U*nlike the pop-up base, which has to be positioned at the hinge of the card, a pop-out base can be positioned anywhere. Make the pop-out base using a strip that folds into five equal sections, not four. Glue the last section, 5 in the illustration, to section 1, forming a square box. Glue this doubled side to the card itself, then glue your cut-out image to section 3.

*A*nother useful kind of base is called a pop-up platform. It's made of two same-size pieces of card (they don't have to be the same color), one glued inside the other. First, fold both cards in half and choose which card will be the inside color.

Make a pop-up platform by cutting two slits across the fold in the card.

This same principal—cutting across the foldline—makes a simple place card with an image that pops up. Flatten the card good side up on the worktable and very lightly draw a line where the fold will be. Stamp the image so it crosses the foldline. Now cut around the part of the image that is above the foldline, using a sharp-pointed X-Acto knife. Erase the pencil line, and score the foldline without scoring through the image. When you fold the card, the image will stand up. Project number 42 features this technique.

Once you get the idea, you will be able to make cut-out images pop up and pop out in many different places, depending on how you measure and fold their bases. You can illustrate stories by making three dimensional scenes with many different pop-ups inside a single card. You can even have one pop-up base on top of another, as long as you always cut on a fold. Just be sure your pop-ups plus their bases stay inside the card when it's closed. They're very fragile, and you wouldn't want to give away the surprise.

To see professional examples of these techniques, along with many clever variations, look in pop-up books for children. You'll also find arts-and-crafts project books featuring pop-ups and pop-outs. Making paper pop-ups is a traditional way of creating holiday scenes for Christmas and Easter.

To make this pop-up, stamp the image across the fold of the card, then cut out the top part.

STAMPING ON FABRIC

Rubber stamps work just as well on smooth-textured fabrics as they do on paper, although you must be sure to use special inks. You can add images to T-shirts and scarves, make table napkins with monograms and holiday motifs, and add personal touches to fabrics you can then use for other craft projects.

Suitable inks include permanent inks, fabric paints, transfer ink, and embossed pigment ink. Each ink requires its own particular method, but the basic techniques of preparing fabric and placing the image are the same for all.

The first step is always to wash and iron the fabric. Use soap or detergent to remove any sizing, but don't add fabric softener. Fabric ink is likely to bleed through, so always work on newsprint and be sure to put a piece of cardboard inside the T-shirt or under the top layer of fabric.

Many fabrics move around too much for easy stamping. An embroidery hoop will help hold delicate fabrics in place. For loose knits, try bonding freezer paper to the back side. It will keep the fabric from stretching and also prevent the ink from bleeding through. Bond the shiny side of the freezer paper to the fabric by ironing at the "synthetics" setting. The paper peels right off when you're done.

Images on stretchy garments like tights may become distorted when you put them on. To compensate, stretch the

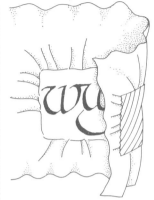

Before stamping on stretchy fabric, prevent distortion by pre-stretching and put tape across the back side. Remove the tape after you stamp the front.

cloth before you stamp it. Hold the stretch while you work by sticking strips of packing tape across the back side.

There are two types of permanent ink for fabrics, water-based and solvent-based. We prefer pads of water-based inks because they're easy to use and easy to clean up. To make the image permanent, cover it with a clean piece of paper and set it with a hot iron. You can also use these inks to make a permanent image that you can watercolor over. Stamp the image onto the paper and heat it to set the ink.

Solvent-based permanent ink comes in ink pads and in dauber-topped bottles.

Pads are best for repetitive stamping of the same color, for borders and backgrounds. The ink dries quickly, so the pad requires frequent re-inking. Use dauber bottles to apply the ink directly to the stamp, more than one color at a time if you like. When you change colors or finish stamping, be sure to remove all the ink from your stamps with a solvent-based cleaner.

𝒻or the greatest range of colors, use water-soluble fabric paints. If you can't find the color you want, you can always mix it. Some paints set by drying, while others need to be heat-set before they can be washed. Apply the colors directly to your rubber stamps using a disposable foam brush; clean stray ink off the stamp with cotton swabs, and when you're done, wash the stamps clean. You can also paint directly onto the fabric, before or after stamping.

𝒮tamping directly onto your new T-shirt doesn't give you much of a chance to practice. To reduce the risks, try using transfer inks. With these special inks, you stamp your design onto any kind of paper, then when you get it right, trans-

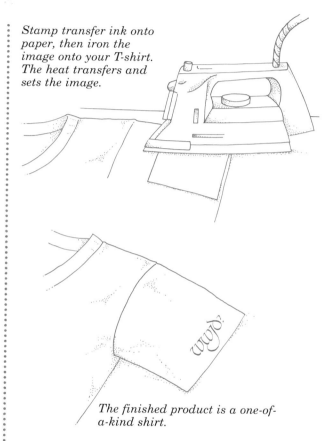

Stamp transfer ink onto paper, then iron the image onto your T-shirt. The heat transfers and sets the image.

The finished product is a one-of-a-kind shirt.

fer it to the fabric by ironing. These inks work best on smooth fabric that contains some polyester. The transfer process reverses the image, so it doesn't work with stamped lettering.

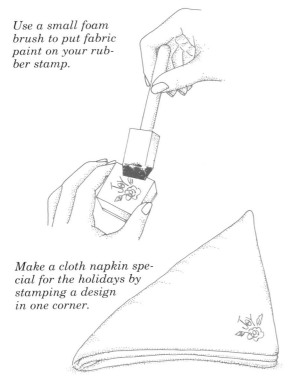

Use a small foam brush to put fabric paint on your rubber stamp.

Make a cloth napkin special for the holidays by stamping a design in one corner.

*U*se fabric glue to attach rhinestones, decorative buttons, and trinkets to your stamped designs. For another kind of embellishment, try fabric puff-paint and glitter pens. These materials become permanent when they dry.

STAMPING ON WOOD

*M*any kinds of paper are made of wood fiber, so permanent inks that work on paper will also work directly on wood. You can make your own woodworking projects, or you can buy attractive boxes and plaques to decorate. Be sure to sand the wood smooth before you stamp on it. Wipe all the sanding dust off with a damp paper towel.

*T*est your colors before you put them on the wood. Even light-colored woods may contain enough pigment to change the colors. Fill in with fabric markers or apply acrylic paints with a brush; let each color dry before you move on to the next. Try using embossing powders, too. They will create some very interesting and unusual effects.

*F*or a more finished look, paint the wood with a solid background before stamping your design on it. After stamping, protect the colors with a clear coat of acrylic finish. Apply the finish in several layers, letting each one dry thoroughly.

Decoupage is the process of gluing colorful printed paper onto wooden objects. Naturally you can make your own paper by stamping, then cut out the images you like and stick them onto smooth wood with ordinary white glue. When the glue dries, fix the images by spraying them with clear acrylic.

Fabric ink and other permanent inks can be stamped on wood. Protect the image and the wood with a spray coat of clear acrylic.

STAMPING ON OTHER MATERIALS

You will find inks formulated for most materials, including plastic, metal, glass, and ceramic. Pigment ink with embossing powder will stick to most materials, though the image may not be very durable. Spray porous surfaces, like clay pots, with clear acrylic before stamping, and also afterward.

MOUNTING STAMPS

Sometimes you will find stamps in the form of rubber dies that have not been mounted on wooden blocks. To mount these stamps yourself, find some kind of block—it can be wood, plastic, or even a small glass jar with a metal lid—and also a foam cushion to put between the die and the mount. Stamp stores sell cushions that are made for mounting stamps, but you can also use craft foam, foam shoe inserts, or a thin rubber mouse pad.

*Trim the rubber die close
to the edge of the image before you glue it onto
the foam cushion.*

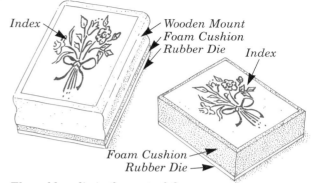

*The rubber die is the part of the
stamp that makes the image. It's glued
to a foam cushion, which is then glued onto
the wooden mount.*

$\mathcal{B}$egin by separating the stamps from one another and by trimming them close to the design. Be careful not to snip into the edge that prints, or to under-cut it. Glue the trimmed stamp onto the foam cushion, using rubber cement. When the glue has set, trim the cushion a little bit larger than the stamp. Stamp the image onto a clean piece of paper and trim and glue this index to the top of the mount. Finally, clean the stamp and glue it onto the block. Orient the stamp the same way as the index you stamped on the top of the block. Otherwise you will not be able to line up the image properly.

MAKING A STAMP

$\mathcal{I}$t's easy to cut a simple shape out of lightweight foam. Use rubber cement to glue the shape onto a block. Another good material is compressed cellulose sponge. Cut out the design you want, then wet the sponge to expand its thickness. Most rubber stamp and craft shops sell a sponge material that's made for stamping. A sponge stamp works with any kind of ink.

$\mathcal{T}$o make a stamp with a lot of detail, carve it into the surface of a large, flat eraser. Cut away the rubber using small craft knives or tools made for cutting

Create your own stamp by carving the image into a large, flat eraser.

linoleum. For safety, you must never push a carving tool toward your hand. Always hold the block so you cut away from your holding hand.

*D*raw your design directly onto the rubber surface. Remember that the rubber you cut away is the part that does not print. The surface that's left is what will pick up the ink. Also, remember that the carved design prints in reverse. To make readable letters, you have to draw them

as mirror images.

*A*n easy way to transfer a design onto the rubber eraser is from tracing paper. Draw the design, blacken the portions of the design you want to print with a soft pencil, then press the paper onto the eraser and rub across the back of the paper with the back of a spoon. This technique allows you to carve letters and words without learning how to write in reverse.

Draw the image on tracing paper, then rub it onto a large, flat eraser.

SPECIAL PROJECTS

STAMP-A-CHRISTIAN GREETING™ SPECIAL PROJECTS

If you have read this far, you have all the information you need to complete the projects shown in full color on the following pages. Instructions for completing these projects come after the colored pages. These projects have been designed to jump-start your creativity. You may choose to follow these instructions precisely, just like a recipe, and recreate the projects for yourself, or you may prefer to just use them as inspiration, a source book of ideas for your own creations.

*H*ave fun, and don't underestimate your own unique creative ability!

USING THE COMPUTER

If you have access to a computer and copier, you can use them to print greetings and messages. This will save you a great deal of tedious copying. Many computer printers will accept card stock, but if yours does not, print your text onto regular paper and copy it onto the card, or glue the paper onto the card.

*M*ost copiers allow you to enlarge or reduce the design. You can tailor many of the projects in this book to your own needs by enlarging or reducing the artwork.

8

11

JESUS
is the
REASON
FOR THE
SEASON

9

Let
Your
Light
Shine

7

Children are a gift from God

psalms 127

10

12

14

13

15

17

16

God took care of Noah.
He'll take care of you too!

18

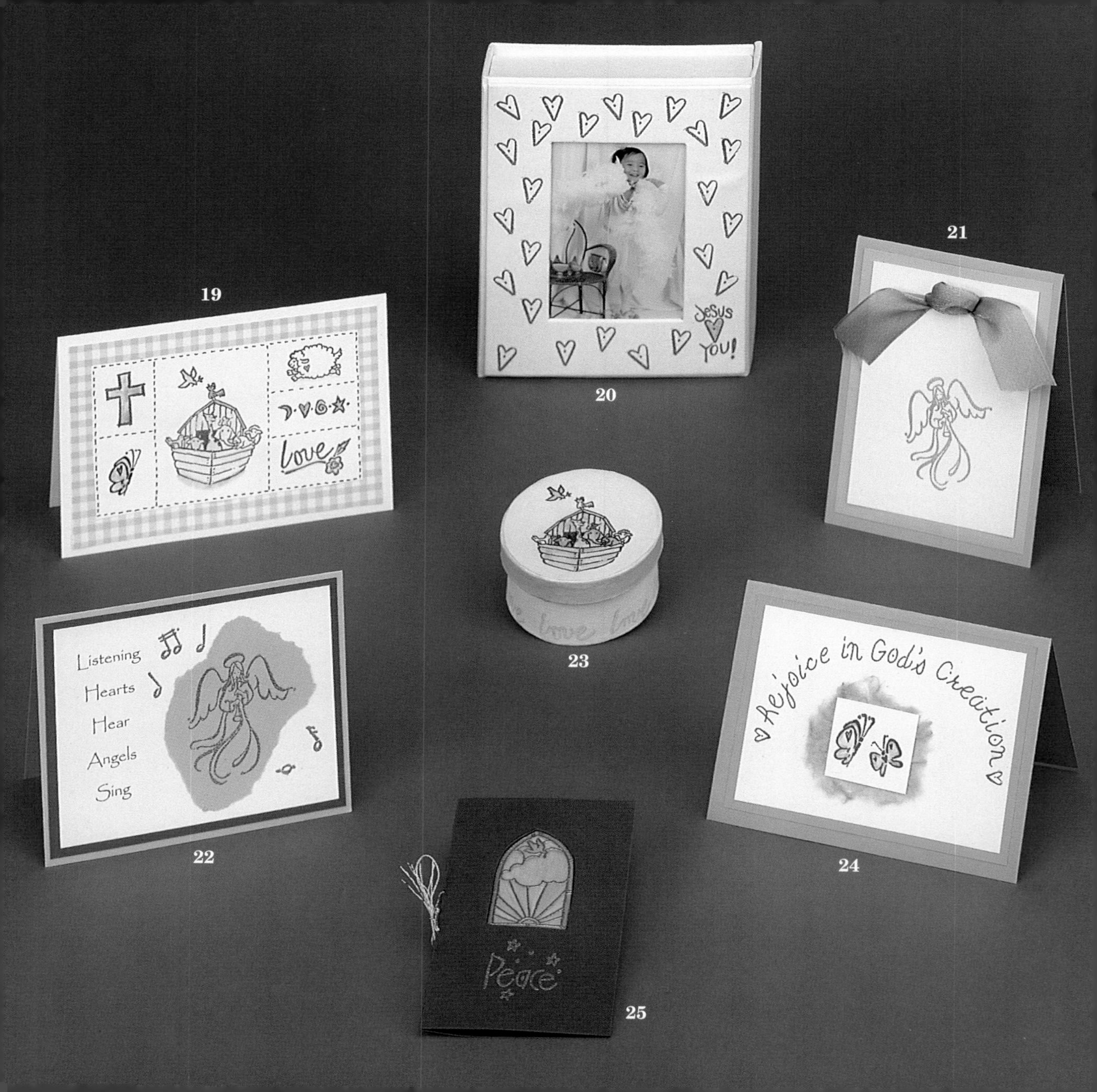
19
Love
20
JESUS
YOU!
21
Listening
Hearts
Hear
Angels
Sing
22
love
23
Rejoice in God's Creation
24
Peace
25

27

26

28

With Thoughts and Prayers

30

saying

a prayer

for you

today

29

love

31

32

Wishing your
baby special
blessings

Happy Christening

33

wwjd?

APRIL 1999

34

Remember —
• Prayer card for Ann
• Flowers

37

Catch the Spirit!

35

Thanks!

36

38

• God heals all •

39

41

Peter Smith

40

Jennifer

43

Jamie Diaz

44

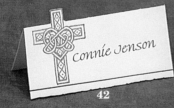
Connie Jenson

42

Sarah Schmidt

46

Lisa Miller

45

47

Rejoice with us
in the birth of
Jennifer Louise Nelson
January 15, 1999
7 pounds 12 ounces
John and Lori

49

wwjd?

48

You're invited to
celebrate with us
John's First Communion
St. Mark's Church
in Newfield

May 16 - 9:00 am

Brunch will be served at our home,
following the service
Walter and Joan Bradley

50

God is Love

51

Love and Faithfulness
Lisa Ann Jones
and
Timothy Wayne Matt

PROJECT NUMBER 1

STAMPS: "Jesus Loves You"

SUPPLIES: White Card, White and Red Card Stock, Black Ink, Double-stick Foam Tape, Decorative-edged Scissors

TIPS & TECHNIQUES: Stamp "Jesus Loves You" using black ink on white paper. Stamp again on white paper, color the heart and cut it out. Use a little snip of double-stick foam tape to float the cut-out heart over the original heart. Now cut out the stamped message and trim the edge with decorative-edged scissors. Draw the large red heart so it resembles the little one, or enlarge the little one on a copier. Glue the red heart on a white card, then use the foam tape to attach the message in the center of the heart.

PROJECT NUMBER 2

STAMPS: "Joy"

SUPPLIES: Precut Photo Card or White Card, Colored Paper, Colored Markers, Black Ink, Ribbon

TIPS & TECHNIQUES: Mount the photo in the photo card, or mount it in a window you cut in a plain card. Choose markers, ribbon, and background paper to match the colors in your photo—we used pink, which comes from the girl's hair ribbon, and blue, from the photo background. Cut a small rectangle from matching card stock. Stamp "Joy" with the cabbage rose in black in the center of the rectangle, then stamp the rose alone on either side. Color the roses and leaves. Glue the stamped image on colored paper, then glue both layers to the card itself. Tie a ribbon in the card's fold.

PROJECT NUMBER 3

STAMPS: Angel, Mini Moon/Heart/ Swirl/ Star

SUPPLIES: White Card, Colored Paper, Metallic Ink or Colored Markers

TIPS & TECHNIQUES: Choose paper in two complementary colors that match your metallic inks or marker colors; we used teal and rose paper, teal metallic ink, and pink metallic ink. Create a frame by stamping the mini designs twice on each side of a square, turn the square up on one corner and stamp the angel into its center. Mount it on matching squares of colored paper and glue the whole assembly onto the white card.

PROJECT NUMBER 4

STAMPS: Grapevine

SUPPLIES: Alphabet Template, Colored Card, White and Colored Card Stock, Black Ink, Colored Markers, Gold Metallic Fine-tipped Marker, Tracing Paper

TIPS & TECHNIQUES: Stencil or hand-letter the message ("God Bless You" in our example), or trace the letters from an alphabet you like. Stamp the grapevine around your message to form a border; we stamped it 12 times. Color the grapevine border, and embellish it with little dots of gold metallic ink. Choose a card and a background paper in colors that complement how you colored the grapevine. Layer the white card onto the colored paper, then glue both of them onto your folded card.

PROJECT NUMBER 5

STAMPS: Lighthouse

SUPPLIES: White and Colored Card Stock, Black, Blue, and Turquoise Ink, Colored Markers, Double-stick Foam Tape, Masking and Sponging Supplies

TIPS & TECHNIQUES: Stamp the lighthouse on white card stock, color it, and cut it out. Locate where the inner white card will fold, ink only the rocks, and stamp them several times. If you like, mask the rocks and stamp more of them to build a bigger pile. Ink the birds and stamp them in the sky and write your message in the sky (we wrote "Let Your Light Shine"). Ink the "water" of the stamp and repeatedly stamp it over the entire bottom half of the card. Make a small cloud mask, then sponge in the sky and water with pale blue. Darken the water by sponging

turquoise into it. Mount the lighthouse, following pop-up instructions on page 70, then glue the inner white card to the green background card.

PROJECT NUMBER 6

STAMPS: Cornucopia

SUPPLIES: Purple Card, Cream and Yellow Card Stock, Colored Pencils, Black Ink, Fine-point Calligraphy Pen, Ribbon, 1/8-inch Hole Punch

TIPS & TECHNIQUES: Stamp and color the cornucopia in the center of a rectangle of cream-colored card stock. Wrap purple ribbon around the card and glue ends on the back side. Mount on yellow card stock and write your message. Punch two holes an inch apart in the center, near the top, thread with ribbon, and tie a neat bow. Mount on a folded purple card.

PROJECT NUMBER 7

STAMPS: Mini Moon/Heart/Swirl/Star

SUPPLIES: Cream Card, Various Colored Papers, Fine-point Calligraphy Pen, Lighthouse Postage Stamp, Brown Ink, Embossing Supplies

TIPS & TECHNIQUES: This card is a collage, and the best arrangement of elements and colors is up to you. Begin by choosing a pri-

mary element or focal point—we started with a postage stamp of a lighthouse, you might find some other picture about light. Choose your colors according to the ones in your image. Stamp the mini star in brown ink on one of the background papers; enlarge the stars by drawing around them. Write your message (we used "Let Your Light Shine") on brown Kraft paper, tear it out, and emboss the torn edges.

PROJECT NUMBER 8

STAMPS: Dove

SUPPLIES: Red and White Card Stock, Clear Transparency Sheet, Red and Green Fine-tipped Markers, Silver Ribbon, Paper Doily, 1/4-inch Hole Punch, Silver Embossing Powder, Silver Cord

TIPS & TECHNIQUES: Make a small bag using red card stock. To make a pattern for the bag, carefully unfold a small brown-paper bag. Use the template to draw and cut a cross-shaped window in the bag. Glue a piece of clear plastic behind it. Fill the bag, fold a doily over the top, and close with a silver bow tied through two punched holes. Make the tag out of white card stock, stamp the dove and emboss it with silver. Draw a fine red line around the dove to frame.

PROJECT NUMBER 9

STAMPS: Mini Moon/Heart/Swirl/Star

SUPPLIES: Green Card, White and Red Card Stock, Metallic Gold Cord, Black Calligraphy Pen, Gold Embossing Powder, Corner Rounder Punch, Embossing Pen, Embossing Supplies

TIPS & TECHNIQUES: Write or print "Jesus is the Reason for the Season" on cream-colored card stock and trim it to size. Punch out the corners with a scallop-shaped corner rounder. String gold cord from corner to corner and anchor on the back. Mount on red paper, then mount on the right side of the green folded card. Stamp the mini star on the left side, and draw around it to create emphasis. Emboss in gold.

PROJECT NUMBER 10

STAMPS: Butterflies

SUPPLIES: White Card, Yellow Card Stock, Black and Metallic Ink, Gold Card, Ribbon, Colored Markers, Fine-point Calligraphy Pen, Double-stick Foam Tape

TIPS & TECHNIQUES: Begin with a folded white card and trim 1/4 inch off the bottom front edge. Glue a yellow card to the inside of the white card, so it shows along the bottom front edge. Cut a second yellow card to the width of the white card, but narrower. Stamp the

butterflies and color them. Cut a square of gold card, tie a ribbon around it, and mount it with the double-stick foam tape. Glue the yellow card onto the white card. Emphasize the edge of the yellow card with a row of dots and dashes. Write your message ("Children are a gift from God"—Psalms 127) on the card.

PROJECT NUMBER 11

STAMPS: Angel, "Joy," Musical Notes

SUPPLIES: White Card, Red Card Stock, Black Ink, White Ribbon with Gold Edges, Colored Pencils, Gold Embossing Powder, Double-stick Foam Tape, Metal Angel Wings, Embossing Supplies, 1/4-inch Hole Punch

TIPS & TECHNIQUES: Stamp musical notes on the front of the white card and emboss in gold. Cut a tag shape from red card stock, stamp twice with "Joy," and emboss in gold. Stamp the angel in black on a scrap of card, color, and cut out, minus wings. Use foam tape to mount the angel on the red tag over the metal wings. Punch a hole through the card and tag, and tie together with ribbon.

PROJECT NUMBER 12

STAMPS: Olive Branch

SUPPLIES: Green Card, White and Yellow Card Stock, Green Ink, Gold Embossing Powder, Embossing Supplies, Decorative-edged Scissors

TIPS & TECHNIQUES: Use the template to draw and cut a cross-shaped mortise mask in scrap paper. Position the mask on a rectangle of white card stock and stamp the olive branch through it in green ink. Trim the edges of the card with deckle scissors and emboss the edges in gold. Mount the white card stock on a larger piece of yellow card stock, then mount both on a folded green card.

PROJECT NUMBER 13

STAMPS: Heart Stencil

SUPPLIES: Brown Kraft Paper, Green Card, Embossing Pen, Gold Embossing Powder, Burgundy Colored Marker, Embossing Supplies

TIPS & TECHNIQUES: Trace two burgundy hearts on a scrap of brown paper, then use the embossing pen to trace a third heart linking the first two. Emboss the third heart with gold, then tear out the shape and emboss its edges. Mount on the green card and glue to the front of a brown folded card.

PROJECT NUMBER 14

STAMPS: Celtic Cross

SUPPLIES: Wrapping Paper, Wide Ribbon, Embossing Pen, Gold Embossing Powder, Corner Rounder Punch, Embossing Supplies

TIPS & TECHNIQUES: Choose your gift wrap

first, then select stamps and colors that go with it. Our paper has stripes of deep green and gold in the background, with muted red motifs and gold outlines. We chose green background paper, a red card, and gold embossing powder. These colors should be more intense than the background, so the design will stand out. The intricate Celtic cross stamp echoes the gold-outlined flowers. To emboss the round-cornered outline, trace around a third piece of card stock.

PROJECT NUMBER 15

STAMPS: Angel

SUPPLIES: Green Card, Dark Purple Corrugated Paper, White or Cream Card Stock, Black Ink Pad, Markers or Watercolor Paints, Gold Metallic Marker, Ribbon Rose, Gold Cord

TIPS & TECHNIQUES: Stamp the angel in black on white card stock and watercolor the image. Color the halo and horn gold, and add gold dots at the tips of the wings. Tear around the image and glue onto the corrugated paper. Tie a piece of gold cord along a valley in the paper, and cover the knot with a ribbon rose. Glue the whole assembly onto a folded card.

PROJECT NUMBER 16

STAMPS: Noah's Ark

SUPPLIES: White or Cream Card Stock, Checkered Background Paper, Muted Gold Card, Black Ink Pad, Colored Pencils, Decorative-edged Scissors

TIPS & TECHNIQUES: Begin with the message, which you can hand-write, stencil, or print from a computer. Then stamp Noah's ark above the message, color it, and cut it out with deckle scissors. Glue the image panel to a larger piece of checkered background paper (ours is brown) and glue that to a folded card.

PROJECT NUMBER 17

STAMPS: Heart with Rose

SUPPLIES: Letter Beads, Black Glossy Card, Red, Silver, and White Card Stock, Silver Embossing Powder, Embossing Supplies

TIPS & TECHNIQUES: String letter beads to spell WWJD, and loop the string through the red paper. Mount on silver paper and then on white or cream-colored card stock. Stamp the three Hearts with Rose and emboss them in silver. Glue the white card onto the face of a folded glossy black card.

PROJECT NUMBER 18

STAMPS: Lamb

SUPPLIES: White or Cream Card Stock, Light-colored Card, Black Ink Pad, Colored Markers, Printed Background Paper, Ribbon, 1/8-inch Hole Punch

TIPS & TECHNIQUES: Choose or computer-print your background paper (ours says "Congratulations!" many times). Stamp the lamb in black on a small piece of white card stock, color its face and feet pink, and its heart to match your colored card. Color the edges of the white card. Layer the white card onto the message paper, then onto the light-colored folded card. Punch the fold for the ribbon and tie a pretty bow.

PROJECT NUMBER 19

STAMPS: Butterfly, Noah's Ark, Lamb, "Love," Mini Moon/Heart/Swirl/Star

SUPPLIES: White or Cream Card Stock, Checkered Background Paper, Colored Pencils, Black Watercolor Ink Pad, Markers or Paints, Black Fine-tipped Pen

TIPS & TECHNIQUES: Stamp the images you want to use on scrap paper and arrange them into neat rectangles. Redraw the rectangles on good paper, using dashes to represent stitch lines. Stamp each image into its own box with watercolor ink. Color the images. To paint with marker inks, lay down a palette by scribbling on a non-porous surface such as plastic, or aluminum foil, then use a small, wet brush to pick up the colors. We have painted a blue shadow under the ark and lamb.

PROJECT NUMBER 20

STAMPS: "Jesus Loves You"

SUPPLIES: Box with Picture Window, Gold Embossing Powder, Colored Markers, Embossing Supplies

TIPS & TECHNIQUES: Stamp and emboss "Jesus Loves You" in the lower right corner of the box. Color the heart red or pink, depending on the colors in your photo. Stamp and emboss the rest of the frame with the heart alone.

PROJECT NUMBER 21

STAMPS: Angel

SUPPLIES: Card Stock in Several Light Colors, Ribbon, Metallic Ink, 1/4-inch Hole Punch, Ribbon

TIPS & TECHNIQUES: Stamp the angel on the lightest color card stock, punch two holes, and loop the ribbon through. Layer it with a complementary color and attach the layered card to a folded card.

PROJECT NUMBER 22

STAMPS: Angel, Musical Notes

SUPPLIES: White or Cream Card Stock, Gold Embossing Powder, Fine-point Black Calligraphy Pen, Embossing Supplies

TIPS & TECHNIQUES: Stamp and emboss the

angel on mauve paper. Tear around the image and glue it to a white or cream-colored card. Write your message along the left side, stacking the words one above the other (ours says "Listening Hearts Hear Angels Sing"). Stamp and emboss several musical notes, then layer on a complementary card color to frame, and attach to a folded card.

PROJECT NUMBER 23

STAMPS: Noah's Ark, "Love" and Rose

SUPPLIES: Round Papier Mâché Box, Cream Card Stock, Colored Markers, Permanent Black Ink, Acrylic Paints, Decoupage Glue/Sealer

TIPS & TECHNIQUES: Use a foam brush to paint the papier mâché box a cream color. Paint the rim of the lid light blue. Brush paint onto the word "Love" from the "Love" and Rose stamp and print it along the bottom of the box. Roll the stamp to follow the curve. Stamp the ark on paper, color it, and cut it to fit onto the box lid. Glue it in place, then seal the paper and the whole box with two coats of decoupage glue.

PROJECT NUMBER 24

STAMPS: Butterflies, Mini Moon/Heart/ Swirl/Star

SUPPLIES: Card Stock in White and Several Colors, Black Ink Pad, Handmade Paper, Colored Markers, Fine-tipped Black Calligraphy Pen

TIPS & TECHNIQUES: Lightly pencil a half circle on white paper, then hand-write, trace, or stencil your message ("Rejoice in God's Creation"). Use a purple marker to ink the heart from the mini designs stamp at each end of the writing. Erase the pencil line. Stamp and color the butterflies on a piece of card stock, mount it on a torn patch of hand-made paper, and layer onto card stock of contrasting colors. Mount onto a folded card.

PROJECT NUMBER 25

STAMPS: Stained-glass Window from Template

SUPPLIES: Vellum Paper, Gold Cord, Dark-colored Card, Gold Embossing Powder, Colored Pencils, Embossing Pen and Supplies, 1/8-inch Hole Punch

TIPS & TECHNIQUES: Trace the stained-glass window onto vellum using the embossing pen. Emboss with gold. Color it with colored pencils. Cut the window shape in the card and mount the vellum behind the cut opening. Write and emboss the word "Peace," then embellish it with stars traced from the template. Punch two small holes in the fold of the card and tie with gold cord.

PROJECT NUMBER 26

STAMPS: Bouquet of Flowers

SUPPLIES: White and Colored Card Stock, Black Brush Marker, Colored Markers, X-Acto Knife, Ribbon

TIPS & TECHNIQUES: Use brush markers to ink the bouquet, but don't ink the ribbon tie. Stamp it on white card stock and color it. Use a sharp knife to make a slit on either side of the bouquet, then thread pink ribbon through the slit and tie a bow. Frame the white card by mounting it on colored stock, then mount everything on a top-folded white card.

PROJECT NUMBER 27

STAMPS: "Joy" with Rose

SUPPLIES: Sheets of White Wrapping Paper or Drawing Paper, Black Brush Marker, Card Stock, Colored Markers, Ribbon, Cord, 1/8-inch Hole Punch

TIPS & TECHNIQUES: Cover the white paper with stamped roses from the "Joy" stamp. Color the roses. Stamp the entire image onto the tag and color it. Tie the tag onto the ribbon bow.

PROJECT NUMBER 28

STAMPS: Lily

SUPPLIES: Purple and Cream Card Stock, Black Ink Pad, Colored Markers, Ribbon, Liquid Pearls, 1/8-inch Hole Punch

TIPS & TECHNIQUES: This layering project requires cutting neat round holes in two pieces of card stock. One way is to put an X-Acto knife in a pencil compass. Before stamping the lilies with waterproof ink, lightly draw a 3-inch layout circle on cream-colored card stock. Test the layout on scrap—we fit nine lilies, all with the flower looking outward. Color the leaves and stems green, then paint the flowers with Liquid Pearls (we used White Opal). The "Happy Easter" message is hand-lettered on the front of the folded white card. To see it, you have to cut a large circle out of the purple background paper. Punch two holes and tie the ribbon before you layer the cards.

PROJECT NUMBER 29

STAMPS: Bouquet of Flowers

SUPPLIES: Cream Card Stock, Paper in Two Complementary Colors, Black Brush Marker, Flower Pot Button, Colored Markers or Stencils, Fine-point Calligraphy Pen, Colored String

TIPS & TECHNIQUES: The folded body of this multi-layered card is a piece of colored paper glued onto one side of the cream-colored stock. Folding the card off center exposes the light inside color, creating a space for your

message. Practice writing your message on scrap, one or two words to a line (ours reads, "Saying/a prayer/for you/today"). Make the image panel by stamping the bouquet on a small piece of light-colored card stock, layered onto a background piece of colored paper. Use a brush marker to ink only the flowers of the stamp. We used a wooden flower pot, which you might be able to buy at a stamp or craft shop. Otherwise, cut the flower pot out of brown cardboard. Tie a string bow around it before gluing it down.

PROJECT NUMBER 30

STAMPS: Lily

SUPPLIES: Teal-colored Deckle-edged Folded Card, Cream Card, Ivory Ribbon, Teal Ink

TIPS & TECHNIQUES: Stamp four teal-colored lilies onto ivory ribbon. Write your message on the cream-colored card (ours says, "With Thoughts and Prayers"). To insert the ribbon into the card, cut two vertical slits above the message. Mount on a teal-colored card.

PROJECT NUMBER 31

STAMPS: "WWJD?", Fish

SUPPLIES: Round Metal-edged Tag with Key Chain, Black Ink, Dusty-Rose Pigment Ink, Clear Embossing Powder, Embossing Supplies

TIPS & TECHNIQUES: Stamp or letter "WWJD?" in black on one side of the circle tag. Stamp the fish on the other in dusty rose, then emboss using clear powder.

PROJECT NUMBER 32

STAMPS: Heart with Rose, "Love" with Rose

SUPPLIES: White Card Stock, Two Complementary Colors of Card Stock, Colored Markers, Black Ink

TIPS & TECHNIQUES: Repeatedly stamp the heart onto white card stock, leaving space for the "Love" with Rose stamp. We stamped ten hearts. Color, then cut out and layer onto the colored card stock, then onto the card.

PROJECT NUMBER 33

STAMPS: Lamb

SUPPLIES: Yellow Card, White Card Stock, Green Printed Background Paper, Black Ink, Colored Markers

TIPS & TECHNIQUES: Write, stencil, or computer-print your message on white card stock (ours says, "Wishing your/baby special/blessings/Happy Christening"). Stamp the lamb three times over the message. Color in the lambs' faces, feet, and hearts; choose colors that match your printed background paper. Layer the message and background paper onto the folded yellow card.

PROJECT NUMBER 34

STAMPS: "WWJD?"

SUPPLIES: Small Calendar, Card Stock in a Dark Shade and Pale Hue of the Same Color, Cream or Ivory Card Stock, Black Ink Pad, Gold Embossing Powder, Embossing Supplies

TIPS & TECHNIQUES: Cut a piece of ivory card stock 2 3/4 inches x 1 3/4 inches and stamp "WWJD?" on it. Cut the edges with decorative-edged scissors, run an embossing pen around the edges, and emboss with gold. Mount the card on a larger piece of dark-colored background card. To make the calendar stand, cut a piece of light-colored card 3 1/2 inches x 11 inches. Score and fold in half, then score 1 1/4 inch in from each end. Cut a 1/2-inch slit in the center of both ends; when you fold the card and interlock the slits, it will stand up. To make it lean back, score a line 1/2 inch above the back bottom fold. Flatten the stand to glue the message cards and calendar onto it.

PROJECT NUMBER 35

STAMPS: Olive Branch

SUPPLIES: Cream or Ivory Card Stock, Colored Ink, Sponge, Fine-point Calligraphy Pen, White Paper

TIPS & TECHNIQUES: Begin by writing the message on white card stock (ours says, "Catch the Spirit!"). To make the crosses, cut a mortise mask (page 40) and sponge over the message. To make the background paper, sponge all over white paper with the same color ink as one of the crosses. Texture the background by stamping the olive branch all over it, in the sponged color.

PROJECT NUMBER 36

STAMPS: Fish

SUPPLIES: Cream or Ivory and Dark-colored Card Stock, Fun Foam or Thin Rubber Mouse Pad, Gold Ribbon, Gold Metallic Ink, Brown Brush Marker, 1/8-inch Hole Punch, Decorative-edged Scissors

TIPS & TECHNIQUES: First, make a square stamp for the gold diamond on the bottom left corner of the ivory card stock. To make the stamp, cut a square of fun foam or thin rubber mouse pad, and glue it onto a wooden block. Stamp the fish in brown ink on top of the gold square. Punch two holes to thread the gold ribbon through, and write the word "Thanks!" under the bow. Mount on dark-colored card stock.

PROJECT NUMBER 37

STAMPS: Celtic Cross

SUPPLIES: Blank Memo Cube, Black Ink Pad, Colored Markers, Gold Metallic Pen

TIPS & TECHNIQUES: Loop rubber bands tightly around a blank memo cube. Ink the stamp well and stamp the Celtic cross on three sides of the cube. Color in with markers and a gold metallic pen.

PROJECT NUMBER 38

STAMPS: Celtic Cross, Fish

SUPPLIES: Black Ink, White Card Stock, Card Stock in Two Dark Colors, Ribbon, 1/4-inch Hole Punch

TIPS & TECHNIQUES: Stamp the cross in black ink on white card stock, color the cross, and cut it out. Layer onto two strips of colored card stock. Stamp the fish all along a length of ribbon. To attach the ribbon, punch a hole near the top of the bookmark.

PROJECT NUMBER 39

STAMPS: "Jesus Loves You"

SUPPLIES: Cream Card Stock, Red Card, Gold Metallic Paper, Fine-point Calligraphy Pen, Gold Embossing Powder, Gold Cord, Small Band-Aid, Embossing Supplies, 1/16-inch Hole Punch, Decorative-edged Scissors

TIPS & TECHNIQUES: On a piece of cream-colored card stock, write the words "God heals all." Trim the card's edges with decorative-edged scissors. Stamp the heart on red paper, emboss it in gold, and cut the heart out. Punch a small hole in the Band-Aid and heart and tie them together with the gold cord. Stick the Band-Aid below the message. Mount the card on gold metallic paper and then onto a folded red card.

PROJECT NUMBERS 40, AND 42 THROUGH 46

STAMPS: Bouquet of Flowers, Cornucopia, Celtic Cross, Butterflies, "Jesus Loves You," Grapevine

SUPPLIES: Card Stock of Various Colors, Colored Markers and Pencils, Black Ink, Purple Ink, Fine-point Calligraphy Pen, Embossing Supplies, Cross Punch, Decorative-edged Scissors

TIPS & TECHNIQUES: Make place cards by stamping and coloring images, and writing names, on light-colored card stock. Layer the card onto variously colored backgrounds. The place cards shown are just a few of many, many possibilities.

PROJECT NUMBER 41

STAMPS: "Love" with Rose

SUPPLIES: Cream Card Stock, Small Folded Box, Black Brush Marker, Silver Ribbon, Colored Markers, Fine-point Calligraphy Pen, Decorative-edged Scissors, Heart Template, Embossing Supplies

TIPS & TECHNIQUES: Write your message on cream-colored card stock (ours says, "I thank God/for every/remembrance/of you"). Use an embossing pen and the template to draw the heart next to the message, and emboss it with silver. Use the "Love" with Rose stamp to print three cabbage roses inside the heart. Color the roses and the heart with markers. Use decorative scissors to cut around the message, up to the edge of the heart. Cut around the heart with regular scissors. Mount the message and attached heart on the red cardboard box. Tie a silver ribbon around one handle.

PROJECT NUMBER 47

STAMPS: Angel

SUPPLIES: Pink or Blue Paper, Pink or Blue Ribbon, Pink or Blue Ink, Pink or Blue Card Stock, Silver Metallic Paper, Vellum 1/8-inch Hole Punch

TIPS & TECHNIQUES: Choose blue or pink according to whether you are announcing the birth of a boy or a girl. Use the envelope pattern on page 103 and enlarge to make a 6-inch square envelope. Cut a 5 1/2-inch square of pink paper and make it into a background by repeatedly stamping with the angel. Use a computer to print your announcement on vellum and cut it out on a 5 1/2-inch square. Punch two holes through both vellum and background squares. Thread

a ribbon through the holes and tie a bow. Seal the envelope with a three-layer panel, with the angel stamped on the top layer. Make the biggest layer of silver metallic paper.

PROJECT NUMBER 48

STAMPS: Celtic Cross

SUPPLIES: Silver Metallic Card, Vellum, Metal Rivets, Silver Embossing Powder, Embossing Supplies

TIPS & TECHNIQUES: Use a computer to print your invitation on vellum, or hand-letter it. Stamp the Celtic cross above the message, using clear embossing fluid, and emboss with silver powder. Punch holes and use the setting tool to rivet the vellum onto silver metallic card stock.

PROJECT NUMBER 49

STAMPS: "WWJD?"

SUPPLIES: Ivory Card Stock, Dark-red Corrugated Paper, Green Handmade Paper, Black Ink, Purple Marker, Heart Template

TIPS & TECHNIQUES: Stamp WWJD? on white paper and use the template with a purple marker to trace a heart over it. Cut out the image. Layer it onto green handmade paper, then onto the dark red corrugated paper, then onto the ivory-colored card.

PROJECT NUMBER 50

STAMPS: Square and Hearts You Make

SUPPLIES: Fun Foam, Purple and Gold Metallic Ink, Fine-point Calligraphy Pen, White Card Stock, Purple Card, Decorative-edged Scissors

TIPS & TECHNIQUES: Fun foam, which you can buy at rubber stamp stores and craft shops, can be cut into shapes for stamping. For this project cut a square, a large heart, and a small heart. Stamp three gold squares, then stamp a purple heart on top of each square. Write your message below the images (ours says "God Is Love"). Embellish the design by stamping several small hearts. Trim the top and bottom edges of the card with scallop decorative-edged scissors. Glue the design onto a folded purple card.

PROJECT NUMBER 51

STAMPS: Dove, Olive Branch

SUPPLIES: Cream or Ivory Card Stock, Silver Embossing Powder, Teal Ink, Silver Cord, Embossing Supplies

TIPS & TECHNIQUES: Use a computer to print names and any other information onto card stock measuring 8 1/2 x 11 inches, then fold the card in half. Use an embossing pen to draw two interlocking circles, and to stamp the dove. Emboss with silver powder. Frame the design by repeatedly stamping the olive branch, using teal ink. Insert the program for the event and tie with silver cord.

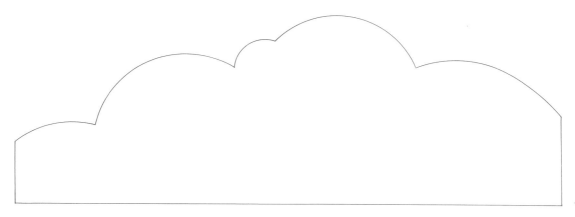

ALPHABET

*Enlarge with a copier
to the appropriate size.*

A B C D E F G H I J K L
M N O P Q R S T U V
W X Y Z ? !

a b c d e f g h i j
k l m n o p q r s
t u v w x y z

SQUARE ENVELOPE

*Enlarge with a copier
to the appropriate size.*

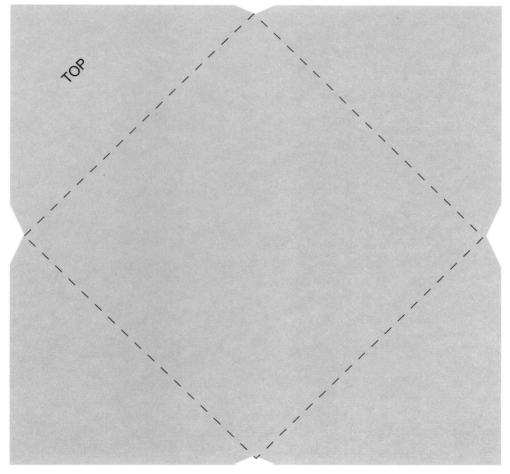

BOX WITH HANDLE

*Enlarge with a copier
to the appropriate size.*

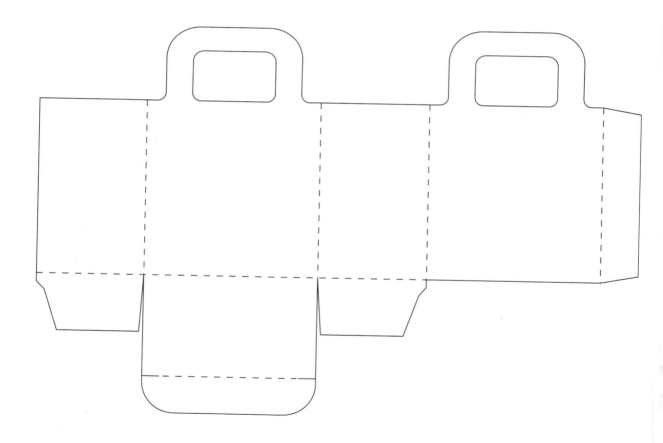